Meditation for the Modern Yogi

in Eight Steps

MEDITATION FOR THE MODERN YOGI

in Eight Steps

LUCY E. JOHNSON

author of YOGA AND SELF-INQUIRY

CONTENTS

Index of Yoga Philosophy Topics

DEDICATION

*In gratitude to B.K.S. Iyengar (1918 to 2014) who
lit the flame of Yoga in many of our hearts.*

SANSKRIT PRONUNCIATION GUIDE

<u>VOWELS</u>

a   f**u**n
ā   c**a**r
i   p**i**n
ī   f**ee**t
u   p**u**t
ū   p**oo**l
ṛ   **r**ig
ṝ   **rea**ch
ḷ   like "lree"
ḹ   same as ḷ but held twice as long
e   pl**ay**
ai   h**igh**
o   **o**ver
au   c**ow**
aṃ   **um**brella
aḥ   ahoy

<u>CONSONANTS</u>

ka   **k**ind
kha   blo**ck**head
ga   **g**ate
gha   Lo**g-h**ut
ṅa   si**ng**
ca   **ch**unk
cha   mat**ch**
ja   **j**ug
jha   he**dgeh**og

ña	bu**n**ch
ṭa	**t**ouch
ṭha	an**t-h**ill
ḍa	**d**uck
ḍha	go**dh**ood
ṇa	thu**n**der
ta	**t**ake
tha	fain**th**earted
da	**d**ate
dha	kin**dh**earted
na	**n**umb
pa	**p**urse
pha	sap**ph**ire
ba	**b**ut
bha	a**bh**or
ma	**m**other
ya	**y**oung
ra	**r**un
la	**l**uck
va	**v**irtue
śa	**sh**ove
ṣa	bu**sh**el
sa	**s**ir
ha	**h**ouse
ksa	wor**ks**heet
tra	**tra**p
jña	"j-nya"

INVOCATION

*To the noblest of sages Patañjali
Who gave us Yoga for serenity of mind
Grammar for purity of speech
And medicine for perfection of the body, I bow
I prostrate before Patañjali
Whose upper body has a human form
Whose arm holds a conch and a disc
Who is crowned by a thousand headed cobra
O incarnation of Ādiśeṣa,
My salutations to Thee*

INTRODUCTION

"Those who aspire to the state of yoga should seek the Self in inner solitude through meditation. With body and mind controlled they should constantly practice one-pointedness, free from expectation and attachment to material possessions." ~ THE BHAGAVAD GĪTA

Dear reader,

In this book I will share with you the necessary tools to establish a daily practice of meditation — the yogic way. I will be presenting these tools in eight steps.

For each step, there is a guided meditation which you can access via a YouTube recording. You will find the link for the guided meditations as we go along.

The guided meditations are there as an extra aid to help you master the practice so that you will eventually be able to do it on your own.

I will also be highlighting some of the fundamental aspects of yoga philosophy that are most relevant to the practice of meditation. This will help you understand these aspects in a deeper and more experiential way, so it is not just a theory for you.

Before we dive into Step 1, we will take a look at some of the commonly asked questions about meditation, as well as a few general practicalities. This is followed by a quick introduction to yoga philosophy.

But first, I'll tell you a little about my spiritual journey up to this point. This will explain how I've been guided to share what I have discovered through my own practice of meditation.

My Spiritual Journey

When I look back upon my life, three instances of feeling touched by grace come to mind.

The first was around the time that I discovered yoga in the late '90s. Wendy, an old university friend, had visited me for the weekend. She had recently been on a retreat at a Buddhist centre in which yoga sessions were offered. I can still picture her demonstrating various postures in my living room. It was fun to also try, and I quickly resolved to find myself a yoga class.

Not long after I began weekly yoga classes in central London, close to my work. The style was 'Iyengar Yoga' named after B.K.S. Iyengar (1918-2014), an Indian teacher of yoga generally credited with popularizing yoga in the Western world. It felt like the perfect method for me as I was stiff and soon discovered that this type of yoga made use of props (such as blocks, belts, and chairs) to help with the various postures.

The moment I felt touched by grace followed within a few weeks later. Whilst browsing in a bookstore during my lunch break, I came across a small section of yoga books. As I reached to take a book from the shelf, I felt from within what I would now refer to as 'atmic power' (the Sanskrit word '*Ātman*' means 'Self'). At that time, I had never heard of terms such as 'Self' or '*Ātman*'. I just assumed it to be a feeling of enthusiasm for my newfound interest in yoga. I bought the book that I had been drawn to, noticing later that day that it was published by the Sivananda Yoga Centre in Putney, South London. I had recently moved to Putney and this centre happened to be within walking distance from my home.

It was at the Sivananda centre that my lifelong interest in Indian Philosophy was born. Over the years that I lived in London I would attend many discourses there.

The second instance of grace felt more significant. My husband was planning a trip to India to attend several days of spiritual discourse in Rishikesh. After some deliberation I had decided to join him. On our first morning in Rishikesh, we happened by chance to walk past Swami Sivananda's cottage ('*kutir*') on the bank of the river Ganges. Swami Sivananda Saraswati (1887-1963), the founder of The Divine Life Society, is widely accepted in India as having been a liberated sage.

As I walked into the area of Swami Sivananda's *kutir*, I was filled with what I can only describe as a huge surge in the 'voltage' or current at the core of my being. Dreams that I'd had in my early days of starting Iyengar Yoga classes came flooding back to me. In one of them I was outdoors practising a seated forward bend. On waking from that particular dream I could vividly recall the physical sensations of my torso resting along my legs (I have still yet to experience this level of proficiency in forward bends!). I had been a bare-chested man in the dream. What struck me most upon waking was the incredible peace of mind I had had whilst holding the dream yoga posture.

Back then I knew very little about the concept of reincarnation. It was during this trip to Rishikesh that it began to dawn on me that the grace of Swami Sivananda had drawn me back, in this life, to yoga and Indian philosophy.

The third and final instance occurred in the summer following my trip to India. I was staying at my in-laws' house on a fairly remote island off the West Coast of Norway. It is an incredibly peaceful place surrounded by majestic mountain peaks and fjords, and the house is sufficiently spacious to provide a private space for morning meditation.

On this particular stay, I found myself slipping more easily into longer periods of deep silence during meditation. One evening after another quiet and contemplative day, just as I went to bed and closed my eyes I felt intoxicated with bliss.

I fell asleep quickly, slipping into a dream where I found myself sitting in front of one of the greatest saints known to India, Sri Ramana Maharshi (1879-1950). He was sitting in silence with his eyes open. There were other people in the dimly lit room; I was situated at the front, quite close to him on his right-hand side. As he began to turn his head toward me, I mentally braced myself unable to block the fear that arose from within, as I instinctively knew what was about to come.

What followed, as his eyes locked onto mine, was a glimpse of Reality that I shall never forget. It remains such a vivid memory. I will try my best to convey with words what happened:

In that instant when Ramana shone his gaze upon me the very Self (my true Essence) that I had been turning towards in deep meditation during the day sucked 'me' into my heart center. I don't really know how it would feel to enter a black hole but that is the best analogy that comes to mind. The intensity was just indescribable as I became an infinite — without any limit whatsoever — ocean of Pure Consciousness-Bliss. For a fraction of a moment I recognized that the entire universe was in me. But even that disappeared.

When recalling this experience after waking-up, the best rational explanation I could think of was that I had full awareness during deep sleep. Sometime later that morning I was struck by the daily message in the Ramana Maharshi Facebook group that I was part of at the time. I cannot remember the exact quote but the gist of it was:

"There is no time and space in the Self. When you understand this, you can get the comfort of a personal visit."

Although this 'touch of grace' occurred in the dream state, it gave me the unshakeable faith that my very Self is that Supreme Reality.

It was shortly after this experience that I took the plunge and retired permanently from working life. Retiring enabled me to dedicate my life wholeheartedly to a spiritual pursuit — a deeper exploration and practice of Yoga as well as the opportunity to take more formal courses in scriptural study of texts such as *The Bhagavad Gītā* and the *Upaniṣads*.

But this book is about you, not me. And the fact that you are interested in meditation and spirituality is proof that grace is already manifest in your life.

The Indian saint Sri Ramakrishna once said:

"The breeze of grace is always blowing on you. You have to open the sails and your boat will move forward."

We open our sails by turning within. This is the art of meditation. Let us now begin this journey together.

COMMONLY ASKED QUESTIONS

- *What exactly is meant by the term 'meditation'?*

Swami Tejomayananda, spiritual leader of the Chinmaya Mission, very aptly defines meditation as the *'effortless awareness of one's true nature'.*

The yogic term we give for one's inner essence or nature is 'Self' or *'Puruṣa'*.

Meditation is the highest spiritual practice, as it is only by turning our attention away from the external world to within that we can realise our true nature — infinite, limitless, and eternal.

This radical shift in attention is described in the *Kaṭha Upaniṣad*:

> *"The Creator made our eyes look outwards, so we see the world outside, not the true inner Self. But a wise sage discovered the inner Self by turning his attention within, seeking enlightenment."*

Before one can meditate on the Self, it is necessary to train the mind to become one-pointed (instead of scattered) by focusing it on something tangible. This is where we will begin in our practice of meditation.

- *Can we be taught (or teach) meditation?*

In a sense, no.

One can be said to be truly meditating only when the mind is one-pointed — when there is effortless focus on the object of meditation. Until that state is reached, one has to make considerable effort to keep dragging the mind back again and again to the focal point of concentration. In yoga, this preliminary stage is referred to as 'concentration'. The state of meditation arises as a result of consistent self-effort in the practice of concentration. It is in this sense that meditation cannot be taught.

But, in another sense — yes.

Fortunately, we can be taught both the necessary preparatory steps for quieting the mind and techniques for concentration. The conscious effort is up to you!

In relation to conscious effort, the practice of meditation rests on the foundation of 'right living': how we interact and behave toward others. Living ethically and morally is key because if we are not, there is little chance that we are able to control the mind and progress on the spiritual path. In yoga, the ethical observances are referred to as '*yamas*' and include the universal vows of non-violence (*ahiṁsā*) and truthfulness (*satya*).

In Patañjali's Yoga of Eight Limbs, *Yama* constitutes the first limb. The 2nd limb, *Niyama,* is a set of personal disciplines such as contentment (*santoṣa*) and study of scriptures (*svādhyāya*).

Together, the *yamas* and *niyamas* help us develop a certain texture of the mind, making it ready for the practice of concentration and meditation (constituting the higher limbs). For example, by the practice of contentment the mind becomes less agitated by wants or needs. By the practice of non-violence in speech, thought and action, anger and greed are minimised.

- *What is the goal of meditation?*

The goal of meditation is the elimination of any kind of suffering for all eternity. This may also be expressed as everlasting and complete fulfilment or happiness, which is one's essential nature.

It takes only a little reflection to recognize that all objects in the external world are impermanent in nature. The joys derived from them are therefore fleeting. Worldly joys are intermixed with doses of pain and suffering, so that suffering comprises an integral part of human life. This is not a negative statement if we consider that suffering provides us with the necessary impetus to seek That which is beyond the temporary!

In yoga, three sources of suffering are traditionally presented:

(i) The pain one experiences because of one's own body and mind, such as disease or mental illness (*ādhyātmika*);

(ii) Miseries caused by other living beings of this world (*ādhibhautika*); and

(iii) Suffering as a result of natural calamities such as floods and earthquakes (*ādhidaivika*).

It is of course impossible to permanently get rid of these various difficulties. The only everlasting solution is to realise the divinity within oneself which is free of all suffering. The nature of the Supreme Self is unsurpassed Bliss. We should not delay in our efforts in putting a permanent end to suffering through the direct realisation of our true nature.

- *Where do the techniques for concentration and meditation originate?*

The methods comprising the ancient science of Yoga were compiled by the great sage Patañjali some 2000 or more years ago. We will see in a later section ('An Introduction to Yoga Philosophy') how Yoga is related to the *Sāṅkhya* School of Philosophy.

Patañjali gave the Yoga System to the world in the form of '*sūtras*' which are short aphorisms or statements, 196 in total. The *Yoga Sūtras* offer us a practical summary of how to achieve deep states of meditation and realise our true nature.

Because the *Yoga Sūtras* are so short and cryptic it is necessary to read them along with a commentary. The first or foundational commentary is by Vyāsa (4th or 5th century). This commentary is known as the Vyāsa *bhāṣya* (*bhāṣya* = commentary). Subsequent commentaries elaborated on the Vyāsa *bhāṣya*, and are treated as an extension of the *sūtras* themselves.

One such commentary is by Swami Hariharānanda Āraṇya (1869-1947), the founder of *Kapil Maṭh*, the only monastery in the world that actively teaches and practices *Sāṅkhya* philosophy. Hariharānanda's commentary is considered to be one of the most authentic and authoritative classical Sanskrit commentaries on the *Yoga Sūtras.*

Practical advice pertaining to meditation is also given in Chapter 6 of *The Bhagavad Gīta*, in which Krishna describes the practice of meditation. *The Bhagavad Gīta*, often called the fifth *Veda*, is one of the most important Yoga scriptures. It is very practical as it teaches us the means to live a spiritual life while in the midst of daily stress, conflicts, and problems.

I will be referring to both of these texts (Patañjali's *Yoga Sūtras* and *The Bhagavad Gīta*) as we go along.

• *Is seated meditation necessary?*

In the West, the practice of yoga is largely centred on various postures. The practice of these postures releases energy blockages in the system and calms the nervous system so that a meditative state is brought about physically, rather than by sitting and watching the mind.

Does this mean we don't have to sit and meditate?

To answer this question, we need to look to the first chapter of Patañjali's *Yoga Sūtras,* where yoga is defined as the control or restraint of the various mental fluctuations. What remains when there is complete cessation of all thought is Pure Being — your true Self. This is the subject of *Yoga-Sūtra* 1.3:

> *"Then the seer [Self] dwells in his own*
> *true splendour."*

To achieve complete cessation of thought — in yoga called *'asamprajñāta samādhi'* — one should have as little body consciousness as possible. For this reason, yoga is best practised in conjunction with seated meditation (or lying down, if you are able to do so without falling asleep!). Yoga postures are a vital aid, but not the necessary means, on the path to *asamprajñāta samādhi.*

• *Does God or religion play a role?*

Although I have laid out the process in steps, meditation should never be considered a mechanical process. Something magical happens when we begin to turn our attention inwards, even quite early on in our practice.

The notion of receiving knowledge of the Self as an act of grace is an ancient one. For example, in the *Kaṭha Upaniṣad* it is said:

*"By the grace of the Creator one perceives the glory
of the Ātman [Self]."*

Although the idea or concept of God may be challenging for many of us in the West, if we are able to add some element of devotion to a higher ideal in our practice, it is a great blessing for us. In doing so we are invoking the Creative grace. Without a sense of reverence or love, meditation can feel dry.

PRACTICALITIES

In order to meditate successfully, some fundamental elements are required such as regularity, a suitable environment, and so on. If you adhere to them, they will help your practice of meditation to be successful.

Regularity, Time, and Environment

- Regularity: practise daily. Do not miss a day. This is very important. You will have good and bad days in your practice but do not let that worry you. Make a firm resolve to continue no matter what. At first the mind will not like meditation; this is normal. After some days, weeks or months of practice, the mind will begin to like it.
- Time: try to practice at the same time every day. Early morning is the ideal time for meditation as you are well rested after a good night's sleep. But early morning is not always convenient because of family commitments, work schedules, and so on. If this is the case, choose whatever time works for your schedule such as afternoon, or early evening.
- Environment: choose a quiet place, perhaps a corner or a room in your house or apartment where you will not be disturbed. To make the place conducive to meditation you may wish to add candle(s), a plant or flowers, an uplifting picture or two. The environment that you create, even if it is in a small area of your home, gives a big support for the mind. The place you choose to meditate will gain a certain spiritual quality or vibration.

Invocation or prayer

When we give an invocation or prayer at the beginning of our meditation, we invoke grace and blessings into our practice. It is by grace that one is able to reach the final destination of the spiritual journey.

For those of us who seek spiritual growth there are several necessary elements. The mind must be disciplined and prepared so that it is capable of discovering the ultimate Truth. We must also have faith (*śraddha*) in both the goal and the means to the goal. But just as importantly, we must have faith in ourselves — that the path is doable for us. The purpose of the invocation or prayer is to ask for help in our meditation and also gain these qualifications.

AN INTRODUCTION TO YOGA PHILOSOPHY

The term 'yoga' comes from the root '*yuj*' which means 'union' or 'to join'.

In its spiritual sense, yoga is the process by which the individual soul becomes united with the Supreme Soul, the Reality that underlies this universe. Yoga may also be defined as the effort to separate the Reality from the apparent.

B.K.S Iyengar expressed this truth as follows in his book *Light on Life*:

> *"There is a universal reality in ourselves [the Self or Ātman] that aligns us with a universal reality that is everywhere."*

That Reality (our true nature) is of the nature of *ananta ānanda* (never-ending Bliss), *parama śānti* (Supreme Peace), Infinite Knowledge, unbroken Joy and Eternal Life. This is the goal of human life.

Geeta S. Iyengar writes in her book *Yoga: A Gem for Women*:

> *"Yoga is the union of the soul with the eternal truth, a state of unalloyed bliss arising from the conquest of dualities. The study of Yoga discipline sharpens the power of discernment and leads towards understanding the true nature of the soul which cannot be fully comprehended by the senses or the intellect alone."*

As Geeta alludes to in the above quote, mere academic study of yoga is futile. The *Yoga Sūtras* have layers of meaning that can only be grasped through practice. There is a beautiful quotation in the *Viṣṇu-purāṇa* that sage Vyāsa includes in his commentary on the *Yoga Sūtras*:

> *"Yoga is the teacher of yoga; yoga is to be understood through yoga. So, live in yoga to realize yoga; comprehend yoga through yoga; he who is free from distractions enjoys yoga through yoga."*

The Orthodox Schools of Indian Philosophy

There are six orthodox schools of Indian philosophy. They are classified as orthodox because they accept the ancient *Vedas* as their source and scriptural authority.

The *Vedas*, of which there are four (*Ṛg, Yajur, Sāma* and *Atharva*), comprise a large body of religious texts composed in Sanskrit. They contain the *Upaniṣads*, dealing with knowledge of the Supreme Self.

In the various scriptures, the Supreme Self is given various names (*Puruṣa, Brahman,* Self, *Ātman,* Spirit, etc.) but each name is referring to the same singular Essence. "Truth is one; sages call it by various names," the *Ṛgveda*, one of India's most ancient texts, declared thousands of years ago.

The six orthodox schools are:

1. ***Yoga*** by Patañjali: Patañjali's Yoga is *Aṣṭāṅga-Yoga* or Yoga of Eight Limbs. Yoga is a methodical effort to control the mind and attain perfection. The system of Patañjali is 'Sa-Īśvara Sāṅkhya' (*Sāṅkhya* with *Īśvara*), because there is *Īśvara* (God or the Lord) in it, who is untouched by afflictions, works, desires, etc. Patañjali built his system on the background of the metaphysics of *Sāṅkhya* but places

great emphasis upon the practical side of self-discipline for the realisation of the *Puruṣa* or true Self.

2. ***Sāṅkhya*** by Kapila: The word '*Sāṅkhya*' means 'number'. The system gives an enumeration of the principles of the universe, twenty-five in number. There is a synthetical system, starting from an original primordial *tattva* or principle, called *Prakṛti*: that which evolves, produces, or brings forth everything else. It is a dualistic system as it assumes the independent existence of *Puruṣa* (the knowing Self) and *Prakṛti* (from which all objects known evolve). Not cognizing the difference between the two is the cause for birth and death. Understanding and being able to cognize the difference between *Prakṛti* and *Puruṣa* gives *mukti* (salvation or final liberation).

3. ***Pūrvamīmāṁsā*** by Jaimini: Concerns the ritualistic portions of the *Vedas*. The aim is to earn merit, leading one to heaven after death.

4. ***Uttaramīmāṁsā*** by Vyāsa: Also called *Vedānta*, this focuses on the philosophical teachings of the *Upaniṣads* rather than the ritualistic portions of the *Vedas*. The *Vedānta* philosophy explains in detail the nature of the Absolute Reality or Supreme Self, and shows that the individual soul is essentially identical to the Supreme Self. It gives methods to remove *avidyā*, the veil of ignorance, and to merge oneself with the ocean of Bliss — the Supreme Reality.

5. ***Vaiśeṣika*** by Kaṇāda: Explains the creation and existence of the universe by proposing an atomistic theory.

6. ***Nyāya*** by Gautama: Concerns theory of logic, methodology and its treatises on epistemology (branch of philoso-

phy concerned with knowledge). The *Nyāya* is sometimes called *Tarka-Vidyā* or the Science of Debate. The *Nyāya* remains the basis of all Sanskrit philosophical studies.

Aṣṭāṅga Yoga (Yoga of Eight Limbs)

The basic premise of the Patañjali's Yoga system is that our perception of the divine Self is obscured by the disturbances of the mind. We are that divine Self already — it is already within us, we just don't see it.

If the mind can be made still, the Self will automatically and instantaneously shine forth.

We have seen above that one of the meanings of the root '*yuj*' (yoke) is 'union'. But there is another very relevant meaning to Patañjali *aṣṭāṅga* yoga and that is 'to control'.

The various methods of the Patañjali *Yoga Sūtras* are given to control the mind and allow access to *sāmadhi*, a state of deep meditation. This leads to direct realisation of one's identity with the Supreme Self and is achieved through the following eight 'limbs':

1. *Yama* — abstentions or moral restraints
2. *Niyama* — observances or disciplines
3. *Āsana* — posture
4. *Prāṇāyāma* — breath control
5. *Pratyāhāra* — withdrawal of the senses
6. *Dhāraṇā* — concentration
7. *Dhyāna* — meditation
8. *Samādhi* — absorption

We will be exploring each of the above limbs as we proceed through the steps of our meditation practice.

Sāṅkhya

As *Sāṅkhya* is the metaphysical framework for Yoga (and the *Yoga Sūtras*), it is helpful for us to have some understanding of its key concepts.

To differentiate between two entities is to be able to tell them apart and ascertain their different nature. Non-differentiation is the opposite — not being able to cognize between the two. As it is the non-differentiation between *Prakṛti* and *Puruṣa* that is the cause for birth and death, and the differentiation between the two that leads to *mukti* (salvation or liberation), we will begin our focus here.

It should be noted that *Sāṅkhya* (and Yoga by association) is a dualistic system, assuming the simultaneous reality of *Puruṣa* and *Prakṛti*, respectively the knowing Self (the 'Seer') and the objects known (the 'seen').

The term 'dualistic' refers to the assumption that they (*Puruṣa* and *Prakṛti*) are two independent realities. Also, according to *Sāṅkhya*, there are many *Puruṣas*.

In contrast, the *Upaniṣads* expound the great truth that the Self or Seer alone is the sole Reality — whatever we happen to call it (*Brahman, Puruṣa*, etc.). And that there is only one Self.

In his book *Raja Yoga* Swami Sivananda assures us:

"Though Raja Yoga [Aṣṭāṅga-Yoga] is a dualistic philosophy and treats of Prakṛti and Puruṣa, it helps the student in Advaitic [non-dual] Realisation of oneness eventually... ultimately the Puruṣa becomes identical with the Highest Self or Brahman of the Upaniṣads.

Raja Yoga pushes the student to the highest rung of the spiritual ladder, Advaitic [nondual] Realisation of Brahman."

In other words, although the framework we are using for spiritual practice is dualistic, it will nonetheless lead us to the realisation of oneness in the end.

The following summary of *Prakṛti, Puruṣa,* and the relationship between them derives from the dualistic system of *Sāṅkhya.*

Prakṛti

Prakṛti means that which is primary, preceding what is made. It comes from *'pra'* (before) and *'kri'* (to make). We can think of it as the primordial material matrix — the very root or ground of this universe and all its objects.

Prakṛti is eternal and all-pervading. It is one. It has no cause but is the cause of all effects. *Prakṛti* is independent and uncaused, while the products or evolutes of *Prakṛti* are caused and dependent.

Prakṛti is composed of three *guṇas* (*sattva, rajas* and *tamas*), like a rope with three strands. *Guṇa* means 'cord'. The *guṇas* are the actual substances or ingredients of which *Prakṛti* is constituted. They make up the whole world evolved out of *Prakṛti*. They are not conjoined in equal quantities, but in varying proportions.

Prakṛti is mere inert matter, but it is equipped with certain potentialities due to the *guṇas*.

Before creation, these three materials or *guṇas* exist in perfect equilibrium and there is no distinction of form or name.

When the balance is disturbed the three materials begin to act on each other, and the result is this universe.

The first to manifest is the cosmic intellect (*buddhi*), also called *Mahat*, in which *sattva-guṇa* predominates. *Mahat* literally means 'the great' as it underpins the entire physical manifestation of the world — the perceivable external universe. We will be revisiting the evolution of *Prakṛti* in Step 4.

The *Sāṅkhya* system is atheistic. It does not accept *Īśvara* (God). The creation produced by *Prakṛti* has an existence of its own, independent of all connection with *Puruṣa*.

Puruṣa

The *Puruṣa* or the Self is beyond *Prakṛti*, and eternally separate from the latter. *Puruṣa* is without beginning or end, without attributes, and without qualities. It is beyond time, space and causality. It is the eternal Seer, perfect and immutable (unchanging). It is also Pure Consciousness (*Cidrūpā*).

The *Puruṣa* is not the doer. It is the Witness. It is not material— it is not a result of combination of the three *guṇas*.

According to *Sāṅkhya*, there are many *Puruṣas* because if the *Puruṣas* were one, all should become free if any one attained release. The different *Puruṣas* are identical in nature. There is no movement for the *Puruṣa*. It does not go anywhere when it attains freedom or release. It remains unchanged.

Each *Puruṣa* remains eternally separate from each other and from *Prakṛti*.

The *Puruṣa* or the Self is the Witness (*Sākṣī*), a spectator (*Draṣṭā*), solitary (*Kaivalya*), and indifferent (*Udāsīna*).

Bondage and release both belong to *Prakṛti* but are attributed to *Puruṣa*. *Puruṣa* is eternally free. Union of *Puruṣa* with *Prakṛti* is the cause of *saṃsāra* or bondage; disunion of *Puruṣa* and *Prakṛti* due to discrimination (differentiation between the two) is emancipation. According to *Sāṅkhya*, release is not merging in the Absolute, but isolation from *Prakṛti*.

GUIDED MEDITATION PRACTICE —
THE EIGHT STEPS

"One ounce of practice is worth a
thousand pounds of theory."
~ Swami Vivekananda

We are now ready to begin the meditation practice.

I recommend that you do not skip any of the early steps, as they build on each other and help train the mind, laying the groundwork for the later steps. This systematic approach will help ensure your success in meditation.

For each step, we will explore various aspects of yoga philosophy. This will not be an exhaustive discussion; that is beyond the scope of this book as the focus here is on the practice of meditation. However, we will look at some of the key ideas that will be helpful to you as you proceed to establish and refine your meditation practice.

In the same way that the meditation practice builds on itself in a step-by-step manner, so too will the philosophy. But it is the meditation practice itself that will help you gain an understanding based on experience. Then it is no longer 'philosophy' but a living reality for you.

I invoke the blessings of our spiritual teachers and predecessors as we now proceed to Step 1.

STEP 1:

GETTING TO KNOW THE MIND

"The yogic journey guides us from our periphery, the body, to the center of our being, the soul. The aim is to integrate the various layers so that the inner divinity shines out as through clear glass."
~ B.K.S. Iyengar

The mind is nothing other than a continuous flow of thoughts.

So, in order to understand and eventually control the mind, we must start by getting to know the various types of thoughts that humans can have. Then we can familiarize ourselves with our own patterns of thinking.

In this step you will practice being the detached observer of thoughts so that you can learn to recognise the different types of mental fluctuations as they arise.

This is a powerful practice because it creates a radical shift in orientation: from being a thinker of thoughts, absorbed by mental activity, to being a detached observer of thoughts.

We will categorize the different mental fluctuations into four types:

PERCEPTIONS

MEMORIES

THOUGHTS

EMOTIONS

For the purpose of the guided meditation, these terms are defined as follows:

- PERCEPTIONS are everything you see, hear, taste, smell, and touch. One's perceptions are conveyed to the mind and experienced as thought.
- MEMORIES are thoughts or mental images arising about the past.
- 'THOUGHTS' here is used in the context of general thinking, mostly in the form of an inner verbal dialogue.
- EMOTIONS are feelings that arise such as joy, irritation, anxiety, sadness, anger, excitement, etc. Emotions may arise in conjunction with any of the other three mental fluctuations. For example: on hearing the sound of birds chirping (PERCEPTION), a feeling of joy may arise; memories of an argument (MEMORY) may give rise to anxiety or anger; and if we happen to start thinking about a future vacation (THOUGHT), excitement may arise in the mind.

STEP 1: Meditation Practise

I now invite you to do the first guided practice with me using this YouTube link:

https://youtu.be/B8_EKQTfhHc
also accessible via
https://www.youtube.com/@TheModernYogiLucy

Alternatively, you may use the written summary given below.

- ❖ Sit comfortably in an upright posture with the head, neck and back in line.
- ❖ Gently close your eyes.
- ❖ Give a silent prayer or invocation asking for help in this meditation.

❖ For some moments simply observe your still, steady posture.

❖ As a detached observer notice any sounds that occur in your external environment. Witness all the different sounds, both near and far. As a sound arises, mentally label it: 'PERCEPTION'.

❖ Also observe the various sensations of the body, such as the contact of the feet on the floor, the touch of the hands on the thighs, and so on. Observe these and any other perceptions you may have. Again, as you observe each perception, mentally label it: 'PERCEPTION'.

❖ As a silent Witness, observe any thoughts, memories, or emotions as they arise in your mind. Label the different mental events as they arise. For example, if a thought of the past arises, mentally label it: 'MEMORY'. Similarly, label any emotions as they arise: 'EMOTION', and label any mental chatter: 'THOUGHT'.

❖ Be completely passive as you observe and label the various mental fluctuations. Do not try and engage with any thought or emotion, etc. Just allow them to come and go.

❖ Continue for ten minutes or so, then start to bring your attention back to the room.

❖ Stretch out your legs, and slowly open your eyes.

STEP 1: Benefits

To prepare for meditation, the very first tool is the capacity to look within and watch the mind. This step will help you to do this with greater ease.

A second important benefit is that if you regularly practise being the passive and detached observer of your mind, you will begin to become more aware of your patterns of thinking in the course of everyday life. This is most helpful for cultivating the five cardinal virtues or '*Yamas*' which constitute the first step of yoga, described below.

Last but not least, this practice helps to create a gap between you and your thoughts. As a result, you will begin to identify less with your thoughts and more with the watchful Presence 'behind' your thoughts.

To the Yoga Scriptures!

In this section, we will look at these fundamental aspects of Yoga philosophy:

- The First Limb of Yoga: *Yama* (abstentions)
- The Second Limb of Yoga: *Niyama* (observances)
- The workings of the mind: *citta* and *citta vṛttis*
- *Saṁskāras* (subconscious tendencies)
- Importance of *sattva guṇa*
- Patañjali's fivefold classification of mental modifications (*vṛttis*)
- The three functions of the *citta*

The First Limb of Yoga: *Yama* (abstentions)

The practice of *Yama* is the practice of right conduct, the very foundation of yoga. The five *yamas* are:

- ❖ *Ahiṁsā* (non-violence): Not causing pain to any creature in any way at any time, in thought, word, or deed. The other *yamas* are given to make this abstention perfect. The practice of *ahiṁsā* will eventually culminate in the realisation of the oneness of all life.

❖ *Satya* (truthfulness): Affirming truth in thought, word, and deed.

❖ *Asteya* (non-stealing): One should be satisfied with what one gets through honest means.

❖ *Brahmacarya* (refraining from sexual misconduct): The yogi will use his or her energies wisely and not overindulge in any sensual pleasure.

❖ *Aparigrahāḥ* (abstinence from greed): freedom from greed or acquisition. The attachment and anxiety accompanying the acquisition and maintenance of possessions are obstacles to quieting the mind.

Spiritual life begins with being a good human being. But being good is not sufficient to reach the goal of yoga. The next (second) limb is required.

The Second Limb of Yoga: *Niyama* (observances)

The five *niyamas* are:

❖ *Śauca* (purity): Purification is of two kinds: internal (mental) and external (physical). Physical purity relates to cleanliness. Internal purity is conquest over negative thoughts such as anger, hate, jealousy, etc.

❖ *Santoṣa* (contentment): Contentment allows the mind to focus, an important ability for practising meditation and other yogic practices.

❖ *Tapas* (austerity): Bringing sincere self-discipline to the practice of the Eight Limbs of Yoga.

❖ *Svādhyāya* (study): Study of scriptures pertaining to Self-knowledge such as *The Bhagavad Gītā, Upaniṣads*, etc. *Svādhyāya* also includes the repetition of *mantras* (sacred sounds) such as *oṁ*.

❖ *Īśvara-praṇidhāna* (devotion to God or Self-surrender). We will explore the significance of this *niyama* in Step 8.

The practice of the *niyamas* removes impurities from the mind. These impurities are twofold: agitations or restlessness; and negativity expressed in thoughts of anger, jealousy, greed, pride, etc. Both types of impurities make the practice of meditation difficult.

The workings of the mind: *citta* and *citta vṛttis*

The name for mind-stuff or substance is '*citta*'. It takes form or shapes which are called '*vṛttis*'.

A common metaphor for the *citta* is a lake. The *citta* is compared to a lake on which waves continuously rise and fall. These waves are thought waves or mental fluctuations (*vṛttis*).

Vṛttis refer to any sequence of thought, ideas, mental imaging or cognitive act.

In the same way that a lake and its waves, ripples, and bubbles are made of water, the *citta*, along with its *vṛttis* are made of the three *guṇas* — *sattva*, *rajas* and *tamas* (see page 20).

When the waves of the lake are stilled, one can see the bottom clearly. Likewise, when the *vṛttis* of the mind subside, one's essential nature becomes evident, and the Self shines forth in undisturbed purity.

In *Yoga-Sūtra* 1.2, this state is called *citta-vṛtti-nirodhaḥ* or cessation of the activities of the mind. In this state the yogi enjoys union with the Supreme Self (*Puruṣa*).

Saṁskāras (subconscious tendencies)

When a *vṛtti* subsides, it leaves an imprint or impression in the subconscious mind. This is known as *saṁskāra*.

A *saṁskāra* of an experience is formed in the *citta* at the very moment that the mind is experiencing something.

All our actions and experiences (good and bad) leave *saṁskāras*, the revival of which induces memory.

Importance of *sattva guṇa*

The three *guṇas* underpin the philosophy of the mind in yoga. Each *guṇa* possesses different attributes:

- *Sattva*: purity, light, harmony
- *Rajas*: passion, activity, motion
- *Tamas*: inertia, darkness, inertness, inactivity

A pure mind (*citta-śuddhi*) is one with almost no *tamas* or *rajas* — *sattva* is what remains.

One of the goals of yoga is to maximize the proportion of *sattva* in the mind and correspondingly decrease that of *rajas* and *tamas*.

This is important because when the mind has cultivated a state of almost pure *sattva*, the discriminative aspect of the mind can reveal the distinction between the *Puruṣu* (Self) and *Prakṛti* (not-Self). A *sāttvic* mind is a peaceful mind with few agitations.

Going back to the metaphor of a lake for the *citta*, agitations in the mind caused by the influence of *rajas-guṇa* are symbolized by the choppy waves in the lake. *Tamas-guṇa* may be compared to mud or sand in the water of the lake. When *tamas* and *rajas* are minimized through the practice of the eight limbs of yoga, what remains is a *sāttvic* mind — one that is like a calm, crystal clear lake.

Patañjali's fivefold classification of mental modifications (*vṛttis*)

Patañjali defines five types of thought waves or *vṛttis*, in *Yoga-Sūtras* 1.6 to 1.11. They are:

1. *Pramāṇa*, right knowledge or right cognition: That which is unquestionably true and reliable. There are three types:

    - *Pratyakṣa*, direct perception: Knowledge experienced directly through the five senses (sound, sight, taste, smell, and touch). For example: tasting an orange or seeing a mountain.

    - *Anumāna*, inference: There may be no physical perception, but right knowledge is arrived at through logic and past experience. For example: one may see smoke and infer that there is a fire.

    - *Āgama*, competent or scriptural testimony: This is knowledge given by scriptures or a person of high character. He or she has had direct experience themselves; their words do not contradict the scriptures; their motives are pure; and the knowledge given is of benefit to mankind.

2. *Viparyaya*, error or mistaken view/wrong knowledge: The real form of an object does not appear. Instead, a false form appears. A classic example is a rope being mistaken for a snake.

3. *Vikalpa*, verbal expression based on imagination without any factual basis: For example, consider the scenario

of spending some time with a friend, afterward imagining that you have hurt their feelings in some way. You spend quite a bit of time thinking over what you said and how your friend may now be displeased with you, only to find out some days later that they have no bad feelings. All your worry and unnecessary thought was *vikalpa* only.

4. *Nidrā*, deep sleep: This manifests when there is a preponderance of *tamas*. In deep sleep there is no knowledge of the external world. When you wake up and say, "I slept soundly; I knew nothing", this means that there must have been a particular kind of subtle wave in the mind during deep sleep.

5. *Smṛti*, memory: Memories arise by recollecting impressions (*saṁskāras*) of past experiences that are embedded in the *citta*.

The three functions of the *citta*

The mind and the intellect are both only thoughts. However, there are functional differences in these thoughts. In yoga, these functions have been classified under the following three categories:

- *Manas* (mind)
- *Buddhi* (intellect)
- *Ahaṅkāra* (ego)

These three divisions are purely functional; they are not organs. An organ is that which has a structure and a function. These three have no structure; they only denote functions.

Manas (mind)

In an experience, the first impact of stimuli from the external world reaches one through the organs of perception — the eyes, ears, nose, etc. For example: when we first look at an object, the image formed on the back of the eye is relayed as an electrical impulse by the optic nerve to the brain. From the brain, it is transmitted to the mind (*manas*). This causes a disturbance in thought, as a result of which there is restlessness and indecision within the *citta*. Thoughts in this condition of doubt or indecision are called the mind (*manas*).

For the intellect to come to a decision about what is perceived, it requires data related to the stimuli received. Such decision-making data is supplied by a function also attributed to *manas* and stems from data that has been stored and accumulated as a result of past experiences. Such stored thoughts are called the memory.

Buddhi (intellect)

After the first impact is over, the disturbance dies down, and quietude is created by one's decision and determination. Thoughts in this condition of decision are called the intellect (*buddhi*).

Ahaṅkāra (ego)

A doubt, a decision, and a memory will be related to each other only if they belong to a single individual. When all of them reside in a person, one is aware that the doubt, the decision and the memory belong to that same person. The constant concept of possessiveness or egoism in feelings of 'I doubt', 'I decide' and 'I remember' is also a thought whose functional name is 'ego'.

Here is an example demonstrating the interactive functions of the *citta*:

If we happen to see an object from far away it might be difficult to decide what the object is. Mind (*manas*) would start thinking and doubting whether the object is a flower or perhaps just a piece of plastic. In order to reach a proper conclusion about the nature of the object, it must be analysed further. So we use intellect (*buddhi*). But the intellect cannot directly come to any final conclusion without first inquiring and comparing with the submerged experiences or storehouse of memories also referred to as the 'subconscious mind'.

If we then happen to come in contact with the object, the intellect now analyses by touch: "it is soft so it is not like paper" or "it has the texture of a petal". The intellect may want further evidence before a conclusion is reached, as there perhaps could be a paper as soft as this. So, it goes again into the subconscious to compare this experience of the object with all other sensual experience lying within the subconscious. It smells the object and compares it with previous experiences. It tastes the object and compares likewise. Intellect says, "it smells and tastes like a flower, but it could still be artificial" (doubting — *manas*).

After diving deep into the subconscious and comparing this experience with thousands already stored there, intellect comes to a conclusion. There is no more thinking and doubting, no more analysing.

Now ego (*ahaṅkāra*) asserts, "I know it is a flower, and not artificial". If, however after searching and comparing, the intellect did not find any similar colour, texture, taste or smell in the subconscious, then the ego would assert, "I do not know".

STEP 2:

WITHDRAWING THE MIND

*"You do not need to seek freedom in a different land,
for it exists within"* ~ B.K.S. Iyengar

You will now learn how to simultaneously withdraw and quiet the mind.

The mind's natural tendency is to be scattered outward, through the senses to the external world of objects.

In order to withdraw and quiet the mind so it is prepared for meditation, it is helpful to do it in stages, gradually taking one's attention from the external to the internal.

The stages that we will apply are: observing external sounds; body awareness; and breath awareness.

You will experience how each of these three consecutive stages progressively quiet the mind, as well as drawing it inwards, away from the external world.

STEP 2: Meditation Practise:
YouTube link for Step 2 guided meditation:

https://youtu.be/A9wm9-elpK0

also accessible via

https://www.youtube.com/@TheModernYogiLucy

- ❖ Sit comfortably in an upright posture, with the head, neck and back in one line.
- ❖ Gently close your eyes.
- ❖ Give a silent prayer or invocation asking for help in this meditation.
- ❖ Take note of your still posture.
- ❖ Be relaxed as you notice all the sounds around you. As a passive Witness, focus only on external sounds.
- ❖ Now begin the process of withdrawing your attention away from the external world, beginning with body awareness. Focus your attention on each and every part of the body, starting with the feet and gradually moving upwards. As you do so, mentally massage that part and relax it.
- ❖ Now turn your attention to your breathing. Without changing your breathing in any way, merely observe the inflow and outflow of the breath, tracing its passage in and out of the lungs.
- ❖ If thoughts arise, do not be carried away by them. As soon as you have noticed that the mind has strayed, bring your focus back to the breath.
- ❖ After five to ten minutes or so of practising breath awareness, slowly bring your attention outward to awareness of the room. Stretch out your legs, and slowly open your eyes.

STEP 2: Benefits

As you practice this technique for withdrawing and quieting the mind you are training the mind to follow your command. This may take quite a bit of effort in the beginning, but do not be discouraged. With practice, it does become easier.

The mind can be compared to an unruly horse. The horse will do anything to try to throw the rider off its back. If the rider manages to remain firmly in the saddle, the horse eventually settles down, accepting the rider as its master.

The mind behaves in exactly the same way; one must take a firm resolve to gain control over it. In the beginning this means dragging the mind back again and again to the focus of concentration, whatever this may be.

In this step you are laying the foundations for a successful meditation practice. In any endeavour, success is rooted in the preparation. If you are preparing for a long journey, it is likely that you will spend some time making the necessary preparations — your passport is up to date, you have your tickets printed, etc. Then the journey is likely to go smoothly. It is the same with the meditation 'journey'. To prepare for meditation, one must first know how to withdraw and quieten the mind.

To the Yoga Scriptures!

In Step 2, we will look at the following aspects of yoga philosophy:

- The Third Limb of Yoga: *Āsana* (posture)
- The five manifestations of the *citta*
- The five *kleśas* (afflictions)
- The Wheel of *Karma*

In the previous step we considered the first two limbs of yoga: *Yama* (abstentions) and *Niyama* (observances). The more we are able to incorporate the *yamas* and *niyamas* into our life, the greater ease we will have at quieting the mind.

We will now look at the Third Limb: *Āsana* (posture).

Although Patañjali's focus is on a seated posture for meditation, this does not mean that the practice of yoga postures is not important. Yoga keeps the physical body in good health, helps prevent many kinds of illness and is invaluable when trying to maintain a still and comfortable posture in meditation.

We will then go on to look at the five manifestations of the *citta*. Finally, we will end this section with a look at the five *kleśas* (afflictions), the underlying cause of the mental fluctuations (*vṛttis*) and how they perpetuate the wheel of *karma*.

The Third Limb of Yoga: *Āsana* (posture)

In chapter 6 of *The Bhagavad Gītā*, Krishna recommends how to set up for meditation:

"In a clean spot, having established a firm seat of his own, neither too high nor too low, made of a cloth, a skin and kusa-grass, one over the other." (Verse 6.11)

In the traditional set-up, a special type of mat made of grass would be placed by the yogi on the ground, providing an insulating effect. Over this, a tiger or deer skin would be laid to give a soft support for the legs and feet. Finally, a cloth or blanket would provide a seat.

We can consider a yoga mat with a blanket laid on top (for softness) and on top of that a meditation cushion or folded blanket(s) as a modern-day equivalent.

Further details of the posture are given in verse 13:

"Let him firmly hold his body, head and neck erect and still..." (Verse 6.13)

The term 'erect' means that the spine, neck and head are

to be in one line. This keeps the energy flowing upward toward the brain, providing alertness.

A suitable posture for meditation, feasible for many, is a simple cross-legged posture. If you are very adept at yoga, you may choose to adopt the full lotus position (*padmāsana*). The key consideration here is that there should be as little body consciousness as possible while you are practising meditation. There should be no discomfort whatsoever in the posture you select. If you are unable to find a suitable seated position on the floor or ground, a chair may be used.

In *Yoga-Sūtra* 2.46, Patañjali uses two words to describe how the posture should be: firm or steady (*sthira*) and comfortable (*sukham*).

Sthira means that once the body is placed in position it should be held still — with no fidgeting. You should be as firm as a statue. There is an intimate connection between the body and the mind, so if the body is unsteady, the mind too becomes unsteady.

But there should also be a degree of comfort. If you are too rigid this will manifest as physical and mental tension.

In summary, the posture that you adopt for meditation is to be erect, but not rigid and relaxed, but not slumped.

The five manifestations of *citta*

In his commentary on the first *Yoga-Sūtra* (1.1), Vyāsa states that at any given time the *citta* may manifest in one of the following forms:

1. *Kṣipta* (scattered or wandering): The mind is restless, its focus scattered on various objects. Such a mind does

not have the patience nor the inclination to focus itself, and finds it difficult to comprehend any subtle principle.

2. *Mūḍha* (dull or forgetful): The mind is infatuated or engrossed in matters connected with the senses such as thoughts of family or wealth. It is unable to think of subtle principles such as the Self.

3. *Vikṣipta* (gathering mind): Most spiritual seekers have this type of mind, which differs from the restless mind (*kṣipta*). One whose mind is of this nature can be calm sometimes and disturbed at other times. When the mind is calm for a certain period, it is able to understand the subtle principles of yoga philosophy and can contemplate on them for some time. There can be concentration with a distracted mind, but it may not last long. The basic trait of this mind is calmness at one time and restlessness at another.

4. *Ekāgrata* (one-pointed): This is a mind which holds onto one thing (object) only. Therein is the state of deep meditation.

5. *Niruddha* (arrested): There is absolute suspension of all mental activity — not a single mental fluctuation (thought or perception).

We will be referring back to these states of mind as we proceed through the steps.

The five *kleśas* (afflictions)

An understanding of the five afflictions (*kleśas*) is important because they are the underlying cause of the *vṛttis* and
the greatest impediments to meditation. The afflictions are:

- ❖ *Avidyā* (spiritual ignorance): This is not knowing one's
  real nature as *Puruṣa*, thus taking the Self to be the
  body and mind.
- ❖ *Asmitā* (ego): The *citta* is mistaken for the sentient Self
  or *Puruṣa*. When you get anger, pain, or joy, you asso-
  ciate yourself with the *vṛttis* and say "I am angry. I am
  miserable. I am happy."
- ❖ *Rāga* (attachment): This is fixation on pleasure or desire for the means of pleasure. It arises through memories of pleasure enjoyed previously.
- ❖ *Dveṣa* (aversion): Through memory of pain, there arises aversion toward both pain and the objects or experiences that give pain.
- ❖ *Abhiniveśa* (clinging to life): This is the strong desire for
  life, or fear of death.

The root affliction is the first one listed above, ignorance
(*avidyā*). The other four afflictions are the effects of ignorance.
If ignorance is destroyed, the other four afflictions will cease
by themselves.

Patañjali (in *Yoga-Sūtra* 2.2) prescribes the performance
of *kriyā-yoga* (yoga of action) for weakening the *kleśas* (afflictions). This consist of three of the *niyamas* (observances): *Tapas*
(self-discipline/austerity); *Svādhyāya* (study of scriptures); and
Īśvara-pranidhāna (dedication of one's actions to God).

For example, through the practice of austerity or self-discipline (*Tapas*), the body and senses are brought under control, weakening the afflictions of attachment (*rāga*) and aversion (*dveṣa*). Through the study of scriptures (*Svādhyāya*), there arises a predisposition to identify less with the body and mind, weakening the afflictions of ignorance (*avidyā*) and ego (*asmitā*). When all of one's actions are performed as a dedication to the Lord (*Īśvara-pranidhāna*), rather than for selfish gain, the result is a tranquil mind that is able to succeed in meditation.

The Wheel of *Karma*

The word '*karma*', from the Sanskrit root '*kri*', signifies action or deed, whether physical or mental (including thought).

Karma is the sum total of our acts, both in the present life and preceding ones.

Karma means not only action, but also the result of action. The consequence is really not a separate thing but is a part of the action.

The law of *karma* is that good (meritorious) actions give rise to *puṇya* (merit) resulting in future happiness in this life or a future birth. Bad actions result in *apuṇya* (de-merit) and future sorrow.

Saṁskāras are subliminal impressions or latent imprints resulting from all of one's actions and experiences.

The sum total of all one's *saṁskāras* is known as *karmāśaya* (stock of *karma*). At the moment of the death, the *karmāśaya* determines the three aspects of rebirth that one will experience: *jāti* (type of birth such as human or animal); *āyuḥ* (lifespan); and *bhoga* (quality of life).

A brief summary of how the *kleśas* operate when they are in full force, perpetuating the wheel of *karma*:

Due to ignorance of one's infinite nature as the Self (*avidyā*), we take ourselves to be this individual body-mind complex (*āsmitā*) with certain likes and dislikes (*rāga/dveṣa*). In our efforts and actions to get what we desire and avoid what we dislike, we perform meritorious or non-meritorious actions giving rise to *puṇya* (merit) and *apuṇya* (de-merit) respectively. *Puṇya* gives rise to future happiness (*sukha*) and *apuṇya* gives rise to future sorrow (*duḥkha*). Our experiences of happiness and sorrow strengthen (and give rise to) our likes and dislikes (*rāga/dveṣa*) leading to further actions. And so, it goes on. This is the wheel of *karma* or cycle of bondage.

The wheel of *karma* comes to a final rest by putting an end to ignorance (*avidyā*). Then *saṁskāras* become like burnt seeds that are unable to sprout, and so the cycle of birth and death comes to an end.

STEP 3:

CONCENTRATING THE MIND

"Do not aim low, you will miss the mark.
Aim high and you will be on the threshold of bliss."
~ B.K.S. Iyengar

The art of meditation begins with concentration, which means placing and fixing one's attention on a chosen object.

In Step 3 guided meditation, the object of concentration is the *mantra* (sacred syllable) *oṁ*, considered to be the most powerful and significant *mantra*.

From ancient times until the present day, spiritual aspirants have used *oṁ* chanting as an aid to meditation. *Oṁ* is accepted as being both one with the Supreme Self and also as the medium connecting the human being to God (*Īśvara*).

You will learn experientially how withdrawal of the mind (*Pratyāhāra*) and concentration (*Dhāraṇā*) go together hand-in-hand. We will gradually withdraw the mind from the external sense objects just as we did in Step 2, in order to turn it toward the chosen object of concentration.

We will use the same Step 2 stages for withdrawing and quieting the mind (observing sounds; body awareness; breath awareness) along with a new, additional stage — that of the 'thought parade' (a term owed to Swami Chinmayananda).

The thought parade stage passively allows any thoughts

to pass by, just as if you were watching a marching band on parade. This allows any thoughts that have already begun to form in your mind to rise to the surface and exhaust themselves. Several minutes of passively observing thoughts — while at the same time being careful not to engage with them and not to generate new thoughts — will help dissipate agitations in the mind. The mind is now available and can turn unimpeded to the object of concentration.

We will chant *oṁ* out loud to begin with, then after some minutes continue with silent (mental) repetition.

STEP 3: Meditation practise

YouTube link for Step 3 guided meditation:

https://youtu.be/5Mjs4Qf8d7I

also accessible via

https://www.youtube.com/@TheModernYogiLucy

- ❖ Sit comfortably in an upright posture, with the head, neck, and back in one line.
- ❖ Gently close your eyes.
- ❖ Give a silent prayer or invocation asking for help in this meditation.
- ❖ Spend a few moments simply observing your still and steady posture.
- ❖ For one or two minutes focus on all external sounds.
- ❖ Body awareness: Focus your attention on each and every part of the body, starting with the feet and gradually moving upwards. As you do so, mentally massage that part and relax it.
- ❖ Breath awareness: Observe the inflow and outflow of

the breath, tracing its passage in and out of the lungs. Continue this stage for two or three minutes.

❖ Thought parade: observe any thoughts, memories, or emotions as they arise in your mind. Be completely passive as you observe the various mental fluctuations. Do not try and engage with any thought. Just allow them to come and go. Continue this stage for a few minutes.

❖ After allowing thoughts to dissipate themselves, begin to chant *oṁ* audibly (pronounced as *Ohhmm*) on each exhalation.

❖ As you continue the chanting, you will notice that the breathing pattern will change and become more rhythmic. Now you can gradually make the chanting of the *mantra* softer and softer until it becomes almost inaudible.

❖ Mentally (silently) chant *oṁ* in your own rhythm, on each exhalation. Continue for five minutes or so.

❖ Bring the chanting to an end, slowly becoming aware again of your external environment. Stretch out your legs, and slowly open your eyes.

STEP 3: Benefits

Practice of this step makes the mind one-pointed.

The natural state of the mind is to be multi-pointed or scattered — thinking about all sorts of random things (see Page 41 for a review of the different states of mind). It is not possible to move directly from this state of mind to one in which there are no thoughts. It must first become one-pointed (*ekāgrata*).

Patañjali defines the one-pointed (*ekāgrata*) state as a mind in which, on the fading away of one thought, the same thought arises again in succession. In the Step 3 guided meditation, this thought is *oṁ*.

Initially as you chant *oṁ*, effort will be required to keep the mind from wandering. The mind will alternate between concentration and being scattered. But this is, in fact, the beginning of concentration.

To the Yoga Scriptures!

In this step we will look at the following aspects of yoga philosophy:

- The Fourth Limb of Yoga: *Prāṇāyāma* (regulation of breath)
- The Fifth Limb of Yoga: *Pratyāhāra* (withdrawal of the senses)
- The Sixth Limb of Yoga: *Dhāraṇā* (concentration)
- The Five Sheaths (*Pañca-kośa*)

In the previous step, we gave attention to the seated posture for meditation. Now we are ready to move to the Fourth Limb of Yoga: *Prāṇāyāma*, which steadies the mind, making it fit for concentration.

We will also look at the composite personality structure of human beings, consisting of the divine spark of life within, called *Puruṣa* or *Ātman* (Self), and the five layers of matter or 'sheaths' enveloping it.

The Fourth Limb of Yoga: *Prāṇāyāma* (regulation of breath)

Prāṇa may be defined as the finest vital force in everything, which becomes visible on the physical plane as motion and action, and noticeable on the mental plane as thought.

It is the same energy (or force) which makes the lungs move (drawing the breath in and out), the heart beat, the earth move and so on. By controlling the movement of the lungs in *Prāṇāyāma*, we are controlling *prāṇa*.

Concentration on one's object of meditation, such as the repetition of *oṁ*, is accompanied by the practice of *Prāṇāyāma*. In the Step 3 guided meditation we chant *oṁ* on each exhalation. This helps the breathing pattern to become slower and more rhythmic.

In the next step (Step 4) we will continue this implementation of *Prāṇāyāma* by incorporating a gentle suspension of breath at the end of each exhalation. This helps to arrest mental fluctuations, enabling the mind to become one-pointed.

There are other breathing techniques which help steady the mind. A particularly helpful one that can be done before meditation practice is alternate nostril breathing. Such techniques are best learnt with the guidance of an experienced teacher.

The Fifth Limb of Yoga: *Pratyāhāra* (withdrawal of the senses)

Pratyāhāra is the conscious turning of one's focus from the outside to inner awareness. This can be done once the mind becomes calm through the practice of *Yama*, *Niyama* and *Prāṇāyāma*.

Pratyāhāra represents the bridge between the external and the internal practises of yoga (see note below). When the senses are withdrawn from objects, then you can fix the mind on a particular point. *Pratyāhāra* and *Dhāraṇā* (concentration) are interdependent. You cannot practice one without the other.

Note: Patañjali considers the first five limbs of yoga (*Yama, Niyama, Āsana, Prāṇāyāma, Pratyāhāra*) to be external limbs and the final three limbs of yoga (*Dhāraṇā, Dhyāna, Samādhi*) to be internal. We can see a gradual progression from the external to the internal. The *Yama* is the most external as it relates to our interactions with other beings — that we should not inflict violence on others or steal, etc. The *Niyama* deals more internally with one's own practices, but still related to external elements, such as cleanliness, contentment with one's situation, etc. *Āsana* focuses exclusively on one's personal body, and *Prāṇāyāma* on the breath within the body. *Pratyāhāra* continues this progression of internalization by going deeper within, withdrawing the senses from objects.

The Sixth Limb of Yoga: *Dhāraṇā* (concentration)

Patañjali defines concentration, *Dhāraṇā,* as fixing of the mind in one place, whether it is external or internal. The mind can be fixed externally on any object, preferably an uplifting one, such as the picture of a saint. But it can be any object you like. Internally it can be fixed on a mental image, or as in Step 3, the silent repetition of a *mantra* (sacred sound).

In *Dhāraṇā*, the effort is to have only one mental fluctuation, *vṛtti* in the mind-lake (*citta*).

The Five Sheaths (*Pañca-kośa*)

The sages of ancient India investigated and established the structure of the personality of human beings.

The *Puruṣa*, or the Supreme Self (*Ātman*), is represented by the sacred, mystic symbol *oṁ*. There are five concentric layers of matter enveloping the *Puruṣa* called '*kośas*' or sheaths.

The *Puruṣa*, veiled by the five sheaths, may be compared to a person wearing five layers of clothes, each layer representing a sheath. Just as the wearer of the clothes lends life to the lifeless clothes when they are worn, the *Puruṣa* or Life Principle provides sentience to the five insentient material layers of the human personality.

The term 'sheath' (*kośa*) indicates that it is a mere covering, having something within itself that is more vital than the covering. Just as the sheath of a sword remains separate from the sword, so too, no real contact exists between the divine spark of life and the matter vestures covering it.

There are five distinct sheaths called *pañca-kośa*. The model of the five sheaths originates from the *Taittirīya Upaniṣad*. They are:

    I. *Annamaya-kośa*, (food sheath)
    II. *Prāṇamaya-kośa* (vital-air sheath)
    III. *Manomaya-kośa* (mental sheath)
    IV. *Vijñānamaya-kośa* (intellect sheath)
    V. *Ānandamaya-kośa* (bliss sheath)

The five sheaths listed above can also be grouped and named differently. They are then referred to as 'three bodies'. We will explore this in a later step.

We will now briefly look at each of the five sheaths in turn:

Annamaya-kośa (food sheath)

The physical body, the outermost layer of our personality beyond which we do not materially exist, is called the food sheath. It consists of muscles, bones, tissues, organs, etc.

It derives the name 'food sheath' from the fact that it has arisen from the essence of food ('*anna*') assimilated by the father, and is nourished in the womb by the food taken by the mother. It continues to exist because of food eaten by the individual and, ultimately, after death it goes back to fertilize the earth and becomes food for other creatures like worms and plants. This physical structure, arising out of food, existing in food, and going back to be food, is thus termed 'food sheath'.

Prāṇamaya-kośa (vital-air sheath)

The fivefold faculties (*pañca-prāṇa*), which correspond to the five main physiological systems, represent the vital-air sheath. The five faculties (*prāṇa*s) comprising this sheath are:

- Faculty of respiration (*prāṇa*): controls the inhalation and exhalation of breath.
- Faculty of excretion (*apāna*): controls the evacuation and rejection of wastes from the body.
- Faculty of circulation (*vyāna*): controls the circulation of blood and thereby the nourishment of body cells and organs.
- Faculty governing reverse processes (*udāna*): controls reverse actions like vomiting, burping and such others. It also facilitates the movement of the subtle body out of the gross body at the time of death.
- Faculty of digestion (*samāna*): this *prāṇa* is in charge of digestion and the assimilation of food and liquids that we take in.

These functions manifest as long as the person is breathing, hence together they are called the *Prāṇamaya-kośa* (vital-air sheath). The vital-air sheath controls and regulates the food sheath, and it can be assumed that the physical body becomes adversely affected when the *prāṇas* (faculties) do not function properly. Physiological activities determine the health and beauty of the anatomical structure.

Manomaya-kośa (mental sheath)

The mental sheath corresponds to the mind and mental activity. It is the part of the mind registering impressions from our sensory apparatus (eyes, nose, ears, etc.) in addition to our basic mental activity, including our emotions.

Vijñānamaya-kośa (intellect sheath)

The intellect sheath corresponds to our experience of intellect, problem solving, intuition and insight. Its qualities include discrimination and decision making.

Ānandamaya-kośa (bliss sheath)

The bliss sheath is the innermost of the five sheaths. It consists exclusively of *saṁskāras*, the imprints of all our experiences.

The deep sleep state, which is the state of ignorance of everything, is the condition in which only *saṁskāras* exist — but without manifestation. The term 'bliss sheath' is derived from the fact that an individual experiences relative bliss during the deep sleep state. In the waking state and dream state, one experiences incessant mental agitation in the mind, but upon reaching deep sleep — whether one is rich or poor, healthy or sick, young or old — one experiences undisturbed peace. This phenomenon occurs because of the total cessation of agitations experienced in the waking and dream states. Hence, the bliss referred to here is a relative experience and it is not to be misunderstood as the infinite Bliss of Self-Realization (*Kaivalya*).

STEP 4:

INTO THE SILENCE

*"When you feel present yet formless, do you not feel
an absence of specific identity? You are there,
but who is there? No one."*
~ B.K.S. Iyengar

In this step you will begin to turn your attention deeper within, to find the divine source of joy, peace and love. This divinity is *Puruṣa*, the Self.

We have seen in earlier steps that the mind is nothing but the flow of thoughts (including memories, emotions, perceptions, etc) and you have by now (hopefully) practised being the passive observer of all your mental fluctuations.

From this practice, you may have made two important observations:

1. Every mental fluctuation (which includes one's thoughts, perceptions, emotions, memories, etc.) is different, but the Witness of all these is one.
2. All thoughts and the rest come and go, whereas the Witness is never not there. It does not come and go.

The Witness is the Self. It is of the nature of Pure Awareness (or Pure Consciousness). And it is You.

In Step 4, the aim of the meditation practice is to begin turning our attention from the object of meditation (the thought *oṁ*) toward the Witness. The technique we shall use is to pay closer attention to the silence in between each repetition of *oṁ*.

We will be incorporating a gentle suspension of breath at the end of each exhalation. You will find this *Prāṇāyāma* technique helpful as it extends the silence in between each *oṁ*.

This step represents a big leap forward in your meditation practice. Therefore, I strongly recommend that you do not rush to Step 5 but continue with the meditation practice given here until you feel completely ready to move on.

STEP 4: Meditation practise

YouTube link for Step 4 guided meditation:

https://youtu.be/5h49mW51wkU
also accessible via
https://www.youtube.com/@TheModernYogiLucy

- ❖ Sit comfortably in an upright posture, with the head, neck and back in one line.
- ❖ Gently close your eyes.
- ❖ Give a silent prayer or invocation asking for help in this meditation.
- ❖ Spend a few moments simply observing your still and steady posture.
- ❖ For one or two minutes focus your attention on all external sounds.
- ❖ Body awareness: Focus your attention on each and every part of the body, starting with the feet and gradually moving upwards. As you do so, mentally massage that part and relax it.
- ❖ Breath awareness: Observe the inflow and outflow of

the breath, tracing its passage in and out of the lungs. Continue this stage for two or three minutes.

❖ Thought parade: Observe any thoughts, memories, or emotions as they arise in your mind. Be completely passive as you observe the various mental fluctuations passing by. Do not engage with any thought; allow them all to pass by. Continue this stage for a few minutes.

❖ Chant *oṁ* audibly three times.

❖ Mentally (silently) chant *oṁ* in your own rhythm, on each exhalation. Continue in this manner for two or three minutes.

❖ Now, as you mentally repeat *oṁ* notice that there is a Witness of the thought *oṁ*.

❖ After each *oṁ*, the Witness alone remains. Observe this.

❖ Gently allow the pause after each exhalation to extend. This will increase the gap between each successive *oṁ*.

❖ Continue repeating *oṁ* for several more minutes, paying attention to the Witness — the awareness that is ever present and unchanging. In the silence between each *oṁ*, just be — remain without thought.

❖ When you are ready, bring the chanting to an end and becoming aware again of your external environment.

❖ Stretch out your legs, and slowly open your eyes.

STEP 4: Benefits

In Step 4 you are moving from quieting the mind to transcending the mind. Focusing on something that is beyond thought is transcending the mind.

The practice of meditation consists of two aspects: quieting the mind and transcending the mind.

Quieting the mind is done by various practises or techniques (such as watching the breath or repeating a *mantra*) It is something we do by our deliberate effort. This first stage is important, but once the mind is quiet the next step is transcending the mind. This is not something we do — it is just remaining, and being.

Step 4 also helps you to begin differentiating the Self from the mind.

To the Yoga Scriptures!

The topics we will look at in Step 4 are:

- The Seventh Limb of Yoga: *Dhyāna* (meditation)
- The Self as Witness
- *Avidyā* (spiritual ignorance) and its solution, *viveka* (differentiation)
- The three bodies: *sthūla-śarīra* (gross body), *sūkṣma-śarīra* (subtle body) and *kāraṇa-śarīra* (causal body)
- The evolution of *Prakṛti* and the twenty-five *Tattvas* (principles)

We will begin this section by looking at the Seventh Limb of Yoga: *Dhyāna* (meditation). As the mind becomes quieter in the meditation practice, you will begin to notice the Silence which is 'behind' the mind. Because it is ever present, illuminating all thought, the Self is described as the 'Witness' (*Sākṣī*).

We will then go on to examine the fundamental affliction of *avidyā*, (spiritual ignorance) — not knowing one's real nature to be Pure Consciousness or Pure Awareness (*Puruṣa*); and the solution — *viveka* (discrimination or differentiation).

We will then explore the three bodies (gross, subtle and causal), also relating them back to the five sheaths we looked at in Step 3. This will help you later to differentiate between the Self and the not-Self.

Finally, we will end this section with a brief look at the creation theory — the evolution of *Prakṛti* as well as the twenty-five *Tattvas* (principles) of classical *Sāṅkhya*.

The Seventh Limb of Yoga: *Dhyāna* (meditation)

Patañjali defines meditation as the continuous flow of similar mental modifications.

He uses the term '*pratyaya*' referring to the image or impression that an object (in this context, the object of concentration) makes on the mind.

When the image of the object of meditation flows uninterruptedly, *eka-tānatā* (in the mind, i.e., without any other distraction) *Dhyāna* has been achieved.

The Sixth Limb of *Dhāraṇā* (concentration) and Seventh Limb of *Dhyāna* (meditation) are not different practices but a deepening of the same practice. In concentration the attention on the object is intermittent or distracted; in meditation, it is unbroken and undistracted. Hence the term *eka-tānatā*, the state of retaining one image in the mind, used to describe meditation.

The Self as the Witness

The Self, *Puruṣa*, is the unchanging Witness — the continuous background of awareness.

In *Yoga-Sūtra* 4.18, it is explained:

"The modifications of the mind are always known to the Self due to the unchanging nature of *Puruṣa*."

Patañjali uses the adjective '*apariṇāmitva*', which means unchanging, to describe *Puruṣa*. Since the Self is eternal, it cannot change. It is not born with the birth of the body, nor does it die with the death of the body.

In contrast, the mind is continuously changing. The churning of thoughts, perceptions, desires, emotions, memories, etc. continuously rise and fall, like endless waves in the ocean.

The Self is distinct from the ever-changing mind. The Witness (subject) cannot be the same as the object (thoughts, memories, etc) it perceives.

Avidyā (spiritual ignorance) and its solution, *viveka* (differentiation)

The mind stuff, *citta*, is made of sufficiently subtle matter that it can reflect or channelise the 'light' of *Puruṣa*.

Puruṣa animates or illumines the inner world of thought or mental space, but the two (*Puruṣa* and the *citta*) are completely distinct entities.

Pure Awareness or Pure Consciousness is the actual animate life force and source of sentiency. The mind, although very subtle, is nonetheless inanimate matter and by itself is inert and insentient.

Animated by reflected consciousness, the mind or *citta* imagines itself to be the real self rather than a material entity external to the Self. This is ignorance (*avidyā*).

Edwin Bryant further explains in his book on the Yoga Sūtras:

"It cannot be overstressed that the mind [citta] is merely a physical substance that selects, organizes, analyses, and molds itself into the physical forms of the sense data presented to it; in and of itself it is not aware of them... only Puruṣa is truly alive, that is aware or conscious.... Pervaded by this consciousness, the citta mind appears as if itself were conscious, as metal placed into intense fire appears as if fire. But the mind animated by consciousness is in reality un-conscious, just as an object appears illuminated in its own right but is in actuality dependent on an outside light source for its illumination and visibility."

The solution to this problem — *citta* imagining itself to be the Self — is *viveka*, the ability to clearly differentiate (cognize) the *Puruṣa* (Self) from the not-Self.

The Three Bodies: *sthūla-śarīra* (gross body), *sūkṣma-śarīra* (subtle body) and *kāraṇa-śarīra* (causal body)

Gross Body, sthūla-śarīra

The term *sthūla-śarīra* means 'gross body'. It is equivalent to the food sheath (*annamaya-kośa*) described earlier. The gross (physical) body is made of skin, flesh, blood, blood vessels, fat, and bones, and has limbs such as the head, hands and legs.

Sthūla, meaning 'gross,' is that which is perceivable by the senses. This gross body is perceived by our senses as well as by those of others, and hence it is called *sthūla*. '*Śarīra*' is that which disintegrates at the time of death.

There are four important aspects of the *sthūla-śarīra*:

1. It is made up of the five gross elements: space, air, fire, water and earth (described in 'The evolution of *Prakṛti*' section below).
2. It is born as the result of good actions of the past. A human embodiment is considered a blessing because only the human species is endowed with the capacity to enquire into the Supreme Truth.
3. It is that by which we experience and interact with the world. The body is often compared to a 'city of nine gates' (*nava-dvāra-pura*) — the two eyes, two ears, the two nostrils, one mouth and the orifices of the anus and the reproductive organ. It is through these that each one of us experiences joys and sorrows and transacts with the world outside.
4. It is subject to the six modifications:
    (i) *Asti* (it exists). This refers to the existence of the body in foetal form.
    (ii) *Jāyate* (it is born).
    (iii) *Vardhate* (it grows). When nourished by food and water, the gross body grows in size.
    (iv) *Vipariṇamate* (it changes). Even after the body attains its full physical maturity it continues to undergo constant changes, discarding old cells, etc. The body also suffers through many diseases and sicknesses which, in turn, produce modifications in it.
    (v) *Apakṣīyate* (it decays). In the course of time, the body slowly starts to weaken, losing its strength and vitality, and we then say that the body has become 'old'.

(vi) *Vinaśyati* (it dies). Finally the body perishes; it disintegrates and becomes one with the five gross elements from which it was created.

Subtle Body, sūkṣma-śarīra

The term '*sūkṣma*' means 'subtle'. Whereas '*sthūla*' (gross) is that which can be perceived by the senses, '*sūkṣma*' is that which cannot be perceived by them. Thus, the very term '*sūkṣma-śarīra*' ('*sūkṣma*'—'subtle'; '*śarīra*'—body) indicates that this subtle body is not an object of sensory perception.

The subtle body is composed of subtle matter or *tanmātras* (described in the next philosophy topic).

The *sūkṣma-śarīra* or subtle body consists of:
- Five *jñānendriyas* (organs of knowledge)
- Five *karmendriyas* (organs of action)
- Five *prāṇas* (vital airs)
- *Manas* (mind)
- *Buddhi* (intellect)
- *Ahaṅkāra* (ego)

The five organs of knowledge are collectively called '*jñānendriyas*' (*jñāna*: knowledge; *indriya*: organ). They are the ear (*śrotram*), skin (*tvak*), eye (*cakṣuḥ*), tongue (*rasanā*) and nose (*ghrāṇa*). Their objects of knowledge are sound (*śabda*), touch (*sparśa*), form (*rūpa*), taste (*rasa*), and smell (*gandha*), respectively.

The five organs of action are collectively called '*karmen-driyas*' (*karma*: action; *indriya*: organ). They are the organ of speech (*vāk*), the hand (*pāṇi*), the leg (*pāda*), anus (*pāyu*) and genitals (*upastha*), whose main functions are, respectively, to speak, to grasp, to enable locomotion, to eliminate body wastes, and to procreate.

The *jñānendriyas* and the *karmendriyas* are not to be construed as the external physical appendages (*golaka*) that can be seen. The physical appendages are part of the *sthūla-śarīra* (gross body). The *jñānendriyas* and the *karmendriyas* are internal (subtle) faculties. Thus, the eye being referred to is the inner faculty of sight and not the external appendage. The external eye (*golaka*) is only an instrument and is not in itself the actual capacity of sight. Say a person loses the outer appendage or *golaka* — the eye, for instance, and is unable to see. This individual has not lost the *jñānendriya*, which is the inner faculty of perception. When the defective *golaka* is set right by surgery or replacement, the inner capacity resumes its function.

The subtle body, which is made up of the senses, mind, intellect and so on, is the instrument through which one comes to enjoy experiences of heat and cold, joy and sorrow, honour and dishonour and so on. Living in the 'house' of the *sthūla-śarīra* (gross body), the individual uses the instruments of *sūkṣma-śarīra* (subtle body) — senses, mind, intellect and so on — to experience the external world of sound, touch, form, taste and smell.

From the standpoint of the *kośa*s, the *sthūla-śarīra* or gross body was described as the *annamaya-kośa* or 'food sheath'. From the very same *kośa* standpoint, the single *sūkṣma-śarīra* (subtle body) is divided into three *kośa*s (sheaths):

(i)   the vital-air sheath (*prāṇamaya-kośa*);
(ii) the mental sheath (*manomaya-kośa*); and
(iii) the intellectual sheath (*vijñānamaya-kośa*).

The five *prāṇas* and the five *karmendriyas* together form the '*prāṇamaya-kośa*' or the 'vital-air-sheath'.

The *manas* and the five *jñānendriyas* (organs of knowledge) together form the '*manomaya-kośa*' or the 'mental-sheath'.

The *buddhi, ahaṅkāra* and the five *jñānendriyas* (organs of knowledge) together form the '*vijñānamaya-kośa*' or the 'intellectual sheath'.

Note that the *jñānendriyas* (organs of knowledge) are common to both the *manomaya-kośa* (mental sheath) and *vijñānamaya-kośa* (intellectual sheath). This is because perceptual knowledge gained through the *jñānendriyas* is vital for the functions of both the *manomaya-kośa* and the *vijñānamaya-kośa*.

Causal Body, kāraṇa-śarīra

The causal body, *kāraṇa-śarīra*, is equivalent to the bliss sheath (*ānandamaya-kośa*). It is made up of *avidyā* (ignorance of the Self) and *saṁskāras*.

Kāraṇa-śarīra is the cause of the *sūkṣma-śarīra* (subtle body, comprising the mind, intellect, etc.) as well the *sthūla-śarīra* (gross or physical body).

Saṁskāras are the impressions of desire and actions entertained by an individual in the past — whether in this present life or from previous lives. The *kāraṇa-śarīra* is the collective repository of these impressions. The *saṁskāras* of the *kāraṇa-śarīra* shape the contours of an individual's temperament and personality determining the individual's nature. They fashion desires and thoughts arising in the mind (*manas*) and govern the course of decisions taken by the intellect (*buddhi*). Hence the *kāraṇa-śarīra* becomes the cause of the *sūkṣma-śarīra* (subtle body).

Each individual is provided a physical body appropriate to his or her cumulative *saṁskāras* alone. Hence the *kāraṇa-śarīra* also becomes responsible for the *sthūla-śarīra* (gross body) that each individual comes to have.

Thus, it is logical to describe the *kāraṇa-śarīra* (causal body) as the cause of the other two *śarīras* — *sūkṣma* (subtle) and *sthūla* (gross).

The *kāraṇa-śarīra* or causal body, apart from being composed of *saṁskāras*, also has the nature of ignorance (*avidyā*). All of us experience this *avidyā* as the absence of Self-Knowledge. In our present state of ignorance, we are unaware of our true nature, which is Pure Consciousness and Absolute Bliss — the complete absence of suffering. This ignorance of the Self's real nature is the unique constituent of *kāraṇa-śarīra*. But for this *avidyā*, we would not have the problem of *saṁsāra* (cycle of birth and death).

Since the *kāraṇa-śarīra*, which is constituted of *avidyā* (ignorance of the Self) and *saṁskāras* (imprints) is beyond the realm of the mind, it is described as '*nirvikalpa*' or 'that which is beyond thoughts'.

The word '*vikalpa*' also has another meaning — 'difference' or 'distinction'. Hence '*nirvikalpa*' means 'without distinction'. Within the *kāraṇa-śarīra*, we do not perceive any visible differences. The *sthūla-śarīra* (gross body) is consitituted of different limbs, such as head, trunk, shoulder and so on and the distinctions between them are clearly seen. In the realm of the *sūkṣma-śarīra* (subtle body) we see that one thought is different from another — the thought of an ice-cream, the thought of a movie and so on. But in the *kāraṇa-śarīra* (causal body), no perceptible difference is perceived between its constituent parts, that is between one *saṁskāra* and another. There are definitely many different kinds of *saṁskāras* in the *kāraṇa-śarīra*, but because they all exist at the causal, unmanifest level, the differences between them are not discernible and they appear homogenous.

The evolution of *Prakṛti* and the twenty-five *Tattvas* (principles)

The *Sāṅkhya* system adopts the theory of evolution and involution: that cause and effect are the undeveloped and developed states of one and the same substance. Cause is a substance in which the effect subsists in a latent form. Just as the whole tree exists in a latent or dormant state in the seed, so also the whole world exists in a latent state in *Prakṛti* — also called the *Avyakta* (unevolved) or the *Avyākṛta* (undifferentiated). There is no real destruction — only involution back into its unevolved and undifferentiated cause. There is a beginningless cycle of evolution ('creation'), maintenance and involution ('destruction').

Under the influence of *Puruṣa*, *Prakṛti* first evolves to produce *Mahat/Buddhi* (cosmic intellect). This first manifestation is like the shoot or sprout from a seed. From *buddhi* comes *ahaṅkāra* (ego).

Ahaṅkāra (ego) has three aspects, all of which are needed in the projection of the world: sāttvika, *rajas*ic and *tāmasa* — also referred to as *vaikṛta, taijasa* and *bhūtādi. Sattva* is responsible for producing the *manas* (mind) and the ten *indriyas* (senses). *Tamas* is the cause of the five *tanmātras* (subtle elements).

The five subtle elements (*tanmātras*) are: *śabda* (sound), *sparśa* (touch), *rūpa* (form), *rasa* (taste) and *gandha* (smell). These are subtle generic energies underpinning sound, touch, form and taste — they themselves cannot be perceived.

The *tanmātras* (subtle elements) grossify, under the effect of *tamas*, into the five gross (and perceivable) elements (*mahābhūtas*) from which the entire physical universe is made. They are: *ākāśa* (space or ether), *vāyu* (air or wind), *tejas* (fire), *āpaḥ* (water) and *pṛthivī* (earth).

The evolution of *Prakṛti* described above requires the help of *rajas*, which has the property of activity or movement (not inherent to either *sattva* and *tamas*). The *rajas*ic aspect of *ahaṅkāra* is required for unfoldment or projection of the *Tattvas*. In this way, the three *guṇas* work together at every level of the projection or manifestation of the universe.

The twenty-five *Tattvas* (principles)

The twenty-five principles (*Tattvas*) according to classical *Sāṅkhya* are summarised below. They are generally accepted as cosmological (as opposed to individual) principles. Separate *Tattvas* are not given for the five *prāṇas* as is the case in other models.

Puruṣa (#1) and *Prakṛti* (#2) are primary. Then from *Prakṛti* there are twenty-three evolutes (#3 to #25) as follows:

Prakṛti first evolves to produce *Mahat/Buddhi* (intellect) (#3), then *Ahaṅkāra* (ego) (#4).

Sixteen further effects emerge from *Ahaṅkāra* (ego):
Manas (the mind) (#5).
Five *Jñānendriyas* (organs of perception) (#6 to #10).
Five *Karmendriyas* (organs of action) (#11 to #15).
Five *Tanmātras* (subtle elements) (#16 to #20).
From the five *Tanmātras* (subtle elements) arise the five *Mahābhūtas* (gross elements) (#21 to #25).
There are no evolutes from *Puruṣa*.

We can see from the above that gross (physical) matter is an evolute or derivative of something subtler, which is an evolute of something subtler still. Cosmic *buddhi* (intellect) or *Mahat* underpins the entire physical world, and each individual human mind is a part of *Mahat*. *Mahat* itself is a manifestation of *Prakṛti* and the three *guṇas*.

From the intellect (*buddhi*) and mind down to physical matter — all is constituted of the three *guṇas*. The *buddhi*, being the finest most subtle material, goes on to become grosser and grosser.

CONSOLIDATION OF STEPS 1 to 4

*"Relinquish your habits and addictions, live a simple
and sober life, don't hurt a living being; this is the foundation
of Yoga. To find reality you must be real in the smallest daily
action; there can be no deceit in the search for truth."*

~ Nisargadatta Maharaj

Before going on to Step 5, I recommend that you take the time to consolidate what you have already learnt, as well as continuing with your regular meditation practice, which now includes the following elements:

- ❖ Steady posture
- ❖ Prayer/invocation
- ❖ Observing external sounds
- ❖ Body awareness
- ❖ Breath awareness
- ❖ Thought parade
- ❖ *Oṁ* chanting
- ❖ Into the silence

You have learnt how the practice of meditation consists of two aspects: quieting the mind and transcending the mind.

Attending to your posture, the first stage, quiets the mind, followed by a short prayer or invocation to set your intent. The body awareness stage quiets the mind even more. Then as you focus on the breath, the breathing becomes still and quiet without effort on your part. When the breath becomes still and quiet, so too the mind. After allowing any surface thoughts to arise and exhaust themselves (thought parade), the object of concentration is introduced, the *mantra oṁ*.

All the elements listed up till here are part of the first aspect of meditation of quieting the mind.

It is in the final stage listed above ('into the silence'), where you now begin to transcend the mind.

Now is a good time, if you haven't already, to begin practicing on your own, without the YouTube recording.

Once you feel ready and are comfortable with the practice, please move on to Step 5.

<u>STEP 5:</u>

TRANSCENDING THE MIND

"You watch yourself from inside.
It is full of Silence." ~ B.K.S. Iyengar

In Step 5 you will continue with the techniques you have learnt for quieting the mind. These remain important elements in our meditation practice. But your focus will now shift to transcending the mind.

To make this inner journey, it is necessary first to quiet the mind. For this, we need to give the mind an object: one thought. Unless we give the mind an object, it will remain scattered.

The single thought or object of focus that we have used in our guided meditation is *oṁ*. Using the technique of chanting *oṁ* we are training the mind to become one-pointed.

In the one-pointed (*ekāgrata*) state there is awareness of only one object. Ultimately, however, we don't want to give the mind any object. To progress in the practice of meditation one must finally give up the object.

In this guided meditation we will practise dropping the object (the single thought *oṁ*).

STEP 5: Meditation practise

YouTube link for Step 5 guided meditation:

https://youtu.be/yq-vu86lBrE

also accessible via

https://www.youtube.com/@TheModernYogiLucy

Begin with the following techniques for quieting the mind that you should now be familiar with:

- ❖ Steady posture
- ❖ Prayer/invocation
- ❖ Observing external sounds
- ❖ Body awareness
- ❖ Breath awareness
- ❖ Thought parade
- ❖ *Oṁ* chanting

Then proceed to the next stage of transcending the mind:

- ❖ As you continue to chant *oṁ*, pay more attention to the Witness, that which is aware of the thought *oṁ*. This awareness is You, the Seer (Self).
- ❖ Put a sudden stop to the chanting. Hold on to this thoughtless state as long as you can.
- ❖ Only the Seer remains.
- ❖ If a thought arises, resume silent chanting.
- ❖ When you are ready, again stop the chanting.
- ❖ Repeat this process one or two more times before bringing the practise session to a close.

STEP 5: Benefits

With practice of this step you will start paying more attention to the nature of Self than your thoughts and emotions. This takes time and consistent effort.

Meditation on the Self not as an object or thought, but as your own being, is the most subtle type of support (*ālambana*) which Patanjali calls '*asmitā*'. From it arises the '*prajña-saṁskara*', the notion that I am the Self, the unchanging Witness.

True meditation — the effortless awareness of one's true nature — is only possible when we understand the nature of the Self.

To the Yoga Scriptures!
The topics we will look at here in Step 5 are:
- The Eighth Limb of Yoga: *Samādhi* (absorption)
- *Saṁyama* (the application of *Dhāraṇā*, *Dhyāna* and *Samādhi*)

These topics are subtle in nature but as your meditation practice matures, you will gain clarity and deeper understanding around them.

The Eighth Limb of Yoga: *Samādhi* (absorption)
We have seen how there is a progression of concentrative absorption on the object of meditation in the Sixth and Seventh Limbs of Yoga. This continues into the Eighth Limb, *Samādhi*, in which there arises effortless one-pointedness for longer periods of time. This is the subject of *Yoga-Sūtra* 3.11:

"The attainment of the Samādhi state involves the elimination of all-pointedness [i.e., wandering] of the mind and the rise of one-pointedness."

The general term for this state is *samprajñāta samādhi*. There is an object of focus or support (*ālambana*) to concentrate the mind. In this state an unwavering image is produced on the concentrated mind (the *pratyaya*).

In *Yoga-Sūtra* 1.17, Patañjali describes a series of progressively subtle levels of *samprajñāta samādhi*. The first (least subtle) level is on an object in the physical universe (*vitarka-samādhi*).

On the second level (*vicāra-samādhi*), the yogi meditates on a subtle object, something that cannot be perceived by the five senses. This includes the subtle universe of potentials called *tanmātras* (see page 69) from which the physical universe has evolved.

The third level of *samādhi* mentioned in this *sūtra* is *ānanda-samādhi*. In his commentary on the *Yoga Sūtras*, Edwin Bryant describes the disagreement among the various classical commentators on what this term means in practice. He writes:

"Vijñānabhikṣu is uncharacteristically vague about this third stage of ānanda-samādhi, although he explicitly disagrees with Vācaspati Miśra. He states that in ānanda-samādhi, the mind transcends the previous stage and experiences bliss due to increase of sattva."

My understanding is that the support (*ālambana*) for concentration in this third stage of *ānanda-samādhi* is the feeling of bliss in the now highly *sāttvic citta*. But this feeling of bliss is only a reflection in the *sāttvic citta* and not the actual Bliss of the Self.

The fourth and most subtle level of *samprajñāta samādhi* is *asmitā-samādhi*. This is not the same as the *kleśa* (affliction) *asmitā* (described on page 43). Swami Sivananda writes in his book, *Raja Yoga*:

"There is only prajña [knowledge] of 'Aham-Tvam' [I am That] in this [asmitā-] Samādhi."

These four levels of *samprajñāta samādhi* are also referred to as *sabīja-samādhi*. *Sa-bīja* means 'with seed'. *Bīja* technically refers to seed in the sense of *saṁskāra*. Any object, even in deep meditation leaves a *saṁskāra* imprint.

There is one more *samādhi*, *asamprajñāta samādhi*, in which there is no support (*ālambana*). We will come back to this in Step 7.

Saṁyama (the application of *Dhāraṇā, Dhyāna* and *Samādhi*)

The primary subject of chapter 3 of the *Yoga Sūtras* is the *siddhis* or mystic powers. These are obtained by performing *saṁyama* on various objects, which is the application of the last three limbs of yoga.

The three processes of *dhāraṇā* (concentration), *dhāraṇā* (meditation), and *samādhi* (absorption) may be practised on any object, external or subtle, at the same time. With the help of these three, the yogi dives deep and gets hidden knowledge and various powers (*siddhis*).

A yogi may perform a 'chain' of *saṁyama*s on the various aspects of one object in order to gain complete knowledge of that object.

Patañjali warns, however, that the powers and knowledge gained are potential obstacles to the goal of yoga as they entice the mind back into the realm of *Prakṛti*.

Ultimately, liberation (*Kaivalya*) can only be gained by turning one's attention to the Self in meditation. This is the most subtle type of support (*ālambana*) for the mind, referred to in the previous section as '*asmitā*'.

This is the subject of *Yoga-Sūtra* 3.35:

"Worldly experience consists of the notion that there is no distinction between Self and sattva (intellect) although these two are completely distinct. Worldly experience exists for another [i.e., for Puruṣa]. [By saṁyama] on that which exists for itself [i.e., on Puruṣa] comes knowledge of Puruṣa."

We have seen already that the first *kleśa* (affliction) of *avidyā* (spiritual ignorance) is confounding the pure Self with the *citta* which moulds itself into the forms and thoughts of this world. Because of this ignorance, the *citta* is unaware that the source of its awareness, *Puruṣa*, is completely distinct from the mental fluctuations that obscure it.

When the mind is quiet and made one-pointed in meditation practice, for example, by chanting a *mantra*, it becomes free of the effects of *rajas* and *tamas*. With practice, the *citta* becomes *sāttvic*, pure and undisturbed like a clean mirror. Now the reflection of *Puruṣa* becomes almost identical to the real *Puruṣa*.

By *saṁyama* on this pure image or reflection in the mind space (the *sāttvic citta*) knowledge of *Puruṣa* arises.

STEP 6:

SELF-INVESTIGATION

*"There is no difference in souls, only the ideas
about ourselves that we wear."* ~ B.K.S Iyengar

In this step you will learn how to separate the Self from not-Self.

The not-Self consists of the five sheaths (or three bodies) — the envelopes of matter that appear to cover your true nature, made up of the three *guṇas*.

How are we to separate the Self from the *kośas* (sheaths) covering it?

The Self is to be recognised by removing the five sheaths. This 'removal' is not to be taken literally. It is impossible to physically remove the *kośas* — the body, *prāṇas*, mind and so on, from the Self. The removal is an intellectual negation; it is of the nature of understanding — 'I am not the five *kośas*'.

This negation process, also referred to as '*Pañca-kośa-viveka*' ('differentiation of the Self from the five sheaths'), is described in the philosophy section below.

A word of caution! Even while negating these sheaths as not-Self, the nature of the Self has to be clearly asserted as Pure Awareness — the Seer or Witness of the five sheaths. If this is not done, one may be led to the erroneous notion that if the Self is none of the sheaths, then the Self must be a non-entity. To avoid this, negation of the not-Self must run parallel with assertion of one's true identity.

There are two important logical arguments that point to the fact that the Self is different from the five sheaths (or three bodies).

1. The sheaths (or bodies) are objects of my knowledge: For the relationship of the witness(er) and witnessed to exist, the witness(er) has to be different from the witnessed. The body, mind, senses and so on are all objects of my knowledge and therefore fall under the category of the 'known' or 'witnessed'. Different from them is the Self, the sole Witness of all five sheaths.

2. The sheaths (or bodies) are known as 'mine': That which is known as 'mine' cannot be me, the Self. When I say 'my car', I remain the possessor of the car and different from it. So too, when I say 'my body', 'my thoughts', 'my hunger', it is evident that the possessor of the body, mind and the *prāṇa*s, has to be different from them.

STEP 6: Meditation practise

YouTube link for Step 6 guided meditation:

https://youtu.be/Siw_pWiUMJw

also accessible via

https://www.youtube.com/@TheModernYogiLucy

Begin with the following techniques for quieting the mind:
- ❖ Steady posture
- ❖ Prayer/invocation

❖ Observing external sounds
❖ Body awareness
❖ Breath awareness
❖ Thought parade
❖ *Oṁ* chanting

Now turn your attention to the various aspects of your human personality. For example:

❖ Body: Your body is constantly changing, yet you know yourself to be the same person that you were when you were a baby, small child, teenager, etc. The Witness Consciousness within (the Self) does not change. The physical body is an object of your perception. You can see, touch, taste, smell and hear it. The Self, therefore, cannot be the body.

❖ Mind: Observe how your mental state is constantly changing. You may be happy one moment, sad the next. Memories, desires, thoughts, and feelings come and go in a never-ending flux. You are aware of thoughts, mental images, feelings, etc., as they arise. These are all objects of knowledge. The Self, therefore, is different from the mind.

If you are not the body or mind, then what are you?

❖ Assert to yourself: I am that Pure Consciousness — the Witness (that which is aware) of the body and mind.

What next?

❖ When a thought arises in the mind, don't be interested in the thought. Be more interested in the Witness of the thought.

❖ Thoughts, emotions, and feeling come and go. But the Witness is constant and unchanging. It does not come and go.
❖ Use any thought or feeling that arises to investigate your true nature, which is unchanging awareness.
❖ After some minutes, when you feel ready, bring the practise session to an end.

STEP 6: Benefits

Viveka — the differentiation (to be able to cognize the difference) between the Self and not-Self, is the direct means to liberation. With *viveka*, one is able to turn towards the Self in meditation.

If *viveka* is strong, *vairāgya* — the natural disinclination towards worldly enjoyments — becomes natural. Because *viveka* points out that everything except the Self is ephemeral, one stops running after the ephemeral. With *vairāgya*, mastery of the mind is automatic.

If *viveka* is weak, *vairāgya* becomes difficult, and control of the mind is not possible.

The method of *Pañca-kośa-viveka* (differentiation of the Self from the five sheaths) described below is truly transformative. But this method is not just for intellectual comprehension. We should try to bring this knowledge in our actual day-to-day life experiences. For example, when you suffer, say with a fever, bring this knowledge to actual use and tell yourself: The body has a fever, not me." Or when the mind is in the grip of desire for a certain object and you are fighting against it, assert your freedom: "This desire does not belong to me; it belongs to the mind." This takes sincere efforts and repeated practice, but you will find that the desire loses its hold on you.

To the Yoga Scriptures!
The topics we will look at in Step 6 are:

- Revision of the five sheaths and three bodies
- *Pañca-kośa-viveka* (differentiation of the Self from the five sheaths)
- *Vairāgya* (dispassion)

Please read the section on *Pañca-kośa-viveka* slowly to give yourself time for reflection. You may also wish to revise what you have learnt so far on the five sheaths and three bodies. For this purpose, a revision summary is provided.

Viveka is also the understanding that the Self alone is permanent and unchanging and everything apart from it is ephemeral. This takes us to the next topic of *Vairāgya* (dispassion).

Revision of five sheaths and three bodies
1. Food Sheath, *Annamaya-kośa* — this is the physical body, composed of the five gross elements, also known as *sthūla-śarīra*.
2. Vital-air Sheath, *Prāṇamaya-kośa*, comprising:
   - *prāṇas* that govern the physiological functions, such as breathing, circulation, and so on.
   - organs of action (*karmendriyas*), the legs and hands, for instance, that enable the motor functions of walking, grasping and so on.
3. Mental Sheath, *Manomaya-kośa*. The following are the constituents of this sheath:

- mind (*manas*).
- sense organs (*jñānendriyas*) — eyes and ears etc.

(4) Intellectual Sheath, *Vijñānamaya-kośa*. The following are the constituents of this sheath:

- intellect (*buddhi*).
- ego (*ahaṅkāra*).
- sense organs (*jñānendriyas*).

The *Prāṇamaya-kośa*, *Manomaya-kośa*, and *Vijñānamaya-kośa* are together called the subtle body, *sūkṣma-śarīra*. The subtle body, made of the subtle elements, has the following 18 aspects:

- Five *jñānendriyas*.
- Five *karmendriyas*.
- Five *prāṇas*.
- *Manas.**
- *Buddhi.**
- *Ahaṅkāra.**

*[Together, *manas*, *buddhi* and *ahaṅkāra* constitute the *citta* ('mind-stuff'). Together, *manas*, *buddhi* and *ahaṅkāra* function as the inner processor of the stimuli received by the *jñānendriyas* and also direct the *karmendriyas* to action.]

(5) Bliss Sheath, *Ānandamaya-kośa* is made up of *saṃskāras* (inherent tendencies) and ignorance about the Self (*avidyā*) and is also called the *kāraṇa-śarīra* (causal body).

Pañca-kośa-Viveka (differentiation of the Self from the five sheaths)

In this methodology, the nature of the Self, which you have hopefully come to understand intellectually by terms such as:

Pure Consciousness (or Pure Awareness); *Nitya* (eternal); Witness of the *kośa*s; *Nirguṇa* (without qualities); *Niṣkriya* (without actions); *Nirvikalpa* (without differences or thoughts); *Nirvikāra* (without modfication), and so on — is now used as criterion to examine whether or not the five sheaths correspond at all to the Self's nature. In this manner, all the *pañca-kośa*s are negated, one by one, to be the not Self.

Negation of *Annamaya-kośa* (food sheath)

The *Annamaya-kośa* or the food sheath is not the Self because:

- <u>The body is impermanent</u>. The body's existence is only for a short time, from its birth to death, at most a span of eighty to a hundred years. The Self is *Nitya* (eternal).
- <u>The body is subject to modifications</u>. During the time span it lives, the body changes from moment to moment. Age, disease, one's lifestyle and many more factors take their toll on the body. The Self is *Nirvikāra* (without modfications).
- <u>The body is inert</u>. The Self is of the nature of Pure Consciousness while the body, being made up of inert substances such as calcium, carbon, etc., is inert in nature.
- <u>The body is an object of my perception</u>. I can see, touch, smell and hear it, whereas the Self, the ultimate Subject, is not an object of perception. It is not possible to see, touch, taste, smell or hear the Self.

For these reasons, I am not the *Annamaya-kośa* (food sheath) and am therefore free from birth, death, disease, age, height, weight, etc., which are all properties of the *Annamaya-*

kośa (food sheath).

Negation of *Prāṇamaya-kośa* (vital-air sheath)

The five *prāṇas* (*prāṇa, apāna, vyāna, udāna* and *samāna*) which govern the various physiological functions such as respiration, evacuation of wastes and circulation of blood along with the five organs of action (*karmendriyas* — the hand, leg, the organ of speech, genitals and anus together) form the *Prāṇamaya-kośa* (vital-air sheath).

The organs of action as well as the *prāṇas* originate from the three *guṇas* and hence are inert in nature. My breath does not know that I practise yoga! In contrast with the *Prāṇamaya-kośa*, the Self has the nature of Pure Consciousness, ever enlivening and illumining all the activities of the *Prāṇamaya-kośa*.

Since I am not the *Prāṇamaya-kośa*, the properties of the *prāṇas* (such as hunger and thirst) as well as the functions of the organs of actions (such as speaking, writing, sitting, running and so on) do not belong to me.

Negation of *Manomaya-kośa* (mental sheath)

The *Manomaya-kośa* or the mental sheath cannot be the Self because:

- The *Manomaya-kośa* has a beginning and an end. The mind arises in the waking state and ceases in deep sleep. But the Self has no beginning nor end.
- The *Manomaya-kośa* is subject to modifications. Desire, fear, excitement, sadness and so on are all the modifications of the mind. Also, the faculties of knowledge, the eyes, ears and so on, grow weak with age.

- <u>I am aware of thoughts, mental images, feelings, and desires as they arise.</u> These are all objects of knowledge. The Self must be different to what is perceives and is, therefore, not the *Manomaya-kośa*.

Negation of *Vijñānamaya-kośa* (intellect sheath)

The *Vijñānamaya-kośa* or the intellect sheath is not the Self because:

- <u>The *Vijñānamaya-kośa* is subject to change *(vikāritvāt)*.</u> The intellect's ideas and ideals often undergo change. The *Vijñānamaya-kośa* is subject to the play of the three *guṇas*. When *sattva*-guṇa is predominant, the intellect is steady, capable of knowledge and intuitive. When *rajas* takes over, the intellect becomes restless and hasty. When *tamas* takes over, the intellect becomes dull and sleepy. As the Self is without changes or modifications (*nirvikāra*), it cannot be the *Vijñānamaya-kośa*.
- <u>The *Vijñānamaya-kośa* is inert.</u> The intellect sheath is essentially inert as it is constituted of the three *guṇas* that are inert in nature. It is only when the light of the Self 'touched' it that the *Vijñānamaya-kośa* becomes sentient and capable of its varied functions — rationalising, differentiating, judging, and so on.
- <u>The *Vijñānamaya-kośa* is an object of knowledge.</u> The intellect is an object of my awareness. I am able to say, 'My intellect was much sharper a few years back'. An object of my awareness can never be the witness Self.

Negation of *Ānandamaya-kośa* (bliss sheath)

The *Ānandamaya-kośa* (bliss sheath) is also an object of my experience.

Deep sleep is a state devoid of thoughts. The mind, intellect and senses are shut down. The mind is now in seed form — in the form of *saṁskāras* that constitute the *Ānandamaya-kośa*. I am aware of neither the physical body nor my thoughts. Yet I, the Witness, remains. After waking up from deep sleep, my sense is that I slept soundly and knew nothing. Deep sleep is an experience of the absence of objects. This proves that the Self is not the *Ānandamaya-kośa*.

Vairagya

In *Yoga-Sūtra* 2.46, Patañjali defines *vairāgya* as:

"That particular state of mind, which manifests in one who does not hanker for objects seen or heard and in which one is conscious of having controlled or mastered those objects, is non-attachment."

Vairāgya (dispassion) is the real strength of the yogi as it helps us to turn within and progress faster in spiritual life.

As long as the mind is prodded with endless desires, the thoughts in the mind will continue to flow out to the various sense objects. A mind extroverted like this will not be available for deep study and continuous Self-investigation. Without in-depth reflections, contemplation on the nature of the Self will be ineffectual and thus the student, even after years of honest efforts, may yet find themselves disappointed by his or her progress.

We can cultivate *vairāgya* by repeatedly bringing to mind that all worldly enjoyments have the following defects:

- They have a beginning and an end.
- They are riddled with pain.
- They dissipate one's energy.
- They leave a sense of incompleteness at the end.
- They create attachment leading to a never-ending cycle of pleasure / memory / pleasure / memory, leading only to increasing disillusionment.

This world and everything in it has a beginning and, therefore, will have an end. Our body, which we mistakenly take to be our Self, is impermanent. The experiences of heat and cold, joy and sorrow that we experience through our body, mind, and intellect are also impermanent. All that is seen, heard, touched, tasted, smelt, felt and known — the whole gamut of our worldly experiences — is fleeting and perishable.

STEP 7:

SHIFTING THE 'I'

*"The Self does not shine in everything although it is
all-pervading. It manifests only in the inner equipment, the
intellect (buddhi), just as the reflection in a clean mirror."*
~ Ādi Śaṅkarācārya

Each of us lives with the assumption that we are limited individuals, and take ourselves to be the body, mind, and intellect. We have lived in this false notion for such a long time that the only antidote is to introduce a new tendency: the thought 'I am the Self, *Puruṣa*'.

It is due to ignorance of the Self that there arises the mistaken notion of the Self as the not-Self, i.e., the identification or the notion of 'I-ness' with regard to the not-Self. This expresses in wrong notions such as: 'I am a man', 'I am a woman', 'This is my father', 'These are my children', 'I am frightened', 'I am sick', 'I am in perfect health', and so on. This false 'I' is termed *ahaṅkāra* or ego.

All these 'I's and 'my's are the expressions of the false 'I'. The truth is that one is neither man nor woman, son nor daughter, calm nor agitated, and sick nor healthy.

This step will help you shift your identification away from the false 'I' to the Self — the true 'I'. Hence the name given of 'Shifting the I'.

STEP 7: Meditation practise

YouTube link for Step 7 guided meditation:

https://youtu.be/KhpFRZOiHhw

also accessible via

https://www.youtube.com/@TheModernYogiLucy

Begin with the following techniques for quieting the mind:
- ❖ Steady posture
- ❖ Prayer/invocation
- ❖ Observing external sounds
- ❖ Body awareness
- ❖ Breath awareness
- ❖ Thought parade
- ❖ *Oṁ* chanting

When you are ready:
- ❖ When a thought rises in the mind, observe it, but with disinterest.
- ❖ Turn towards that which is aware of the thought, the Witness or Seer. As you do so, drop the thought.
- ❖ Assert: I, the pure Self does not get involved in any activity. It is the mind that thinks, imagines, and desires. I do not do any of that. I am the Pure Self. Pure Awareness is my true nature.
- ❖ Now drop even this thought.
- ❖ Turn your attention inward away from the world, body, and mind (all mental activity) and toward awareness.
- ❖ Relax as you give attention to awareness alone.

❖ If thoughts come, do not try to complete them, just turn your attention back to the Self.

What next?

❖ Just be. Without doing. Remain attending to the Self, in effortless awareness of your true nature.

❖ If thoughts arise, again, turn to the Witness of the thought and assert your true nature.

STEP 7: Benefits

With consistent daily practice of Step 7, you will become increasingly grounded in the (discriminatory) knowledge that:

My true nature is Pure Awareness (or Pure Consciousness). As the timeless Self, I am not the body-mind-intellect. Birth, death, health, illness, race are all based upon and exist with reference only to the body. Experiences of joy and sorrow are determined by the mind, and as I am not the mind, they too are not mine at any time.

When this discriminatory knowledge between the Self and not-Self becomes truly grounded and uninterrupted it is referred to by Patañjali as '*viveka-khyāti*' (discriminatory knowledge). In the same manner that *Pratyāhāra* is the bridge linking the first four limbs of Yoga (*Yama, Niyama, Āsana, Prāṇāyāma*) to the last three limbs (*Dhāraṇā, Dhyāṇā, Samādhi*), *viveka-khyāti* is the bridge which will take us from meditation to final liberation (*Kaivalya*).

We have seen that the art of meditation has two aspects: quieting the mind and transcending the mind. When we stop the doing (the very necessary part of quieting the mind at the beginning of our practice) and turn towards the Self, away from all thought, the mind becomes very quiet.

As the mind becomes quiet, the Self become more evident in the mind space. The source of one's sentiency or awareness in the mind space is the *Puruṣa* itself — the Pure (Original) Consciousness. You are That (Original Consciousness).

Eventually the mind becomes so quiet that it stops altogether.

To the Yoga Scriptures!

The topics we will look at here in Step 7 are:
- *Prajñā* (truth bearing wisdom)
- *Viveka-khyāti* (uninterrupted discriminative knowledge)
- *Asamprajñāta Samādhi*
- *Kaivalya* (Liberation)

Prajñā (truth bearing wisdom)

When the *citta* is free from the effects of *rajas* and *tamas*, in other words it is pure and undisturbed, it becomes luminous and clear. At this point the *sāttvic* potential is at its maximum.

The *citta* when pure acts like a spotless mirror, reflecting the face gazing at it without distortion.

In this luminous state, the *citta* can reflect *Puruṣa*'s real image. As a result, knowledge (*prajñā*) of the *Puruṣa* emerges.

Prajñā (truth bearing wisdom or Self-knowledge) produces a certain type of *saṁskāra* of its own, which blocks the activation of the other, conventional, *saṁskāras*. The conventional *saṁskāras* produce only mundane thoughts. As the conventional *saṁskāras* become blocked, one's meditation (*Dhyāna*) deepens into *asmitā-samādhi* (see page 78) in which one remains in effortless awareness of one's true nature.

While this is not the higher (a*samprajñāta*) *samādhi*, by turning towards this pure image or reflection in the seat of meditation, the yogi is one step from *Kaivalya*, complete liberation.

Viveka-khyāti (uninterrupted discriminative knowledge)

Discriminative knowledge is the constant inquiry into the nature of all things — discernment between the Seer (observer) and the Seen (observed), between the Self and not-Self, between the eternal and the non-eternal — until it becomes habitual and permanent. Only when discriminative knowledge is uninterrupted, not only in yoga practice or the seat of meditation, but also in daily life, is liberation viable.

How do we do this?

First, become clear in your understanding that you are not the body and mind.

In contrast, the Self has the nature of Pure Consciousness (or Pure Awareness). It is the very core of one's personality and is ever the Witness (unaffected knower) of the not-Self: the three bodies or five sheaths.

Identify yourself with the all-pervading Eternal Self. Stand as a Witness (*Sākṣī*) of all experiences. Know that the Self is always like a king — distinct from the body, organs, vital breaths, mind, intellect, ego, and *Prakṛti* — the Witness of their attributes.

Begin to put this this into practice in your everyday thought processes:

Since I am distinct from the not-Self (three bodies or five

sheaths), it naturally follows that the qualities of the not-Self cannot affect me, the pure Self, *Puruṣa* and the Witness of the five sheaths. For example: my mobile phone may be broken, but 'I' remain unbroken because I am different from my phone; my house may be on fire, but I am not burnt by the fire which consumes my house because I am distinct from my house.

So too, whether the physical body (*Annamaya-kośa*) is young and healthy or old and sickly, it has nothing to do with 'me', the Self, who am different from the body. Since the body alone has birth and not me, I am not bound by any of the relationships that accrue from the birth of the body. Hence, I really have no mother and no father, am not a spouse, have no children and am neither a mother nor a father nor anyone's child.

Hunger and thirst are expressions of the *Prāṇamaya-kośa* (vital-air sheath) in distress. As I am different from the *prāṇas*, hunger and thirst do not belong to me. Energy and lethargy are also the properties of the *Prāṇamaya-kośa*. From the angle of my real nature, I am neither energetic nor lethargic.

If the thoughts are irresolute and indecisive, still because 'I', the Self, am different from the thoughts, it follows that there is no indecisiveness in me, the Self. Indecisiveness, confusion, or dilemma are only on the plane of the *Manomaya-kośa* or mental sheath.

When the thoughts are decisive, that does not improve my (Self's) status. I remain free from the thought-flux, as I am distinct from the *Vijñānamaya-kośa* (intellectual sheath) also. Whatever resolution or decisiveness occurs, does so at the level of the intellect alone, that is on the plane of the

Vijñānamaya-kośa.

And finally, I am different from the *Ānandamaya-kośa* or the bliss sheath. Even the blissful ignorance of deep sleep state is an object of my (Self's) awareness and hence I am different from the blissful ignorance of the deep sleep state. As I am beyond the pale of *Ānandamaya-kośa* (*kāraṇa-śarīra*), there are no *saṁskāras* (tendencies) in me. I have neither *puṇya* (good tendency) nor *apuṇya* (sinful tendency).

Asamprajñāta Samādhi

When the highest (*asamprajñāta*) *samādhi* manifests, *citta* and all its images and ideas fade away, leaving the Self alone. The means to *asamprajñāta samādhi* is *paravairāgya* (supreme renunciation).

In *asamprajñāta samādhi*, the awareness of *Puruṣa* is no longer aware of any external entity at all, including the *citta* which is, as if, non-existent.

As the awareness or consciousness of *Puruṣa* is no longer being channelled through the *citta* at this point, no *saṁskāras* (seeds) are planted in the *citta*, not even the *prajñā-saṁskāras* described above. *Asamprajñāta samādhi* is therefore referred to as '*nirbīja*', without seed. The *vṛttis* of the mind exist simply as potential and the *saṁskāras*, the subconscious imprints that trigger thoughts, memories, etc., are also latent.

In his book *Raja Yoga*, Swami Sivananda states:

"When the Yogi has reached the last perfect stage of meditation and Samādhi, the fire whereof burns all the residue of his actions. He at once gets liberation in this very life."

Only one experience of *asamprajñāta samādhi* may not be sufficient to result in final liberation. In the next section, we will examine what is meant by the term '*Kaivalya*' in yoga and how this — the highest goal, is reached.

Kaivalya (Liberation)

Patañjali tells us in *Yoga-Sūtra* 2.26 that the means to liberation (*Kaivalya*) is uninterrupted discriminative knowledge (*Viveka-khyāti*). It is knowledge alone that destroys ignorance (*avidyā*) resulting in liberation. *Yoga-Sūtra* 2.25 states:

"By the removal of ignorance, conjunction [between Puruṣa and Prakṛti] is removed. This is the absolute freedom of the seer."

For this, the *saṃskāras* (latent impressions) have to be completely destroyed. Otherwise, thoughts may arise from the old remaining *saṃskāras*. Only when all the *saṃskāras* are wiped out can there be continuous knowledge without a break. Swami Sivananda explains further in his book *Raja Yoga*:

"The vṛttis that manifest in the internal, lose their force and energy gradually and become like burnt seeds and so do not trouble the Yogi. The old vāsanās [saṃskāras] should be completely destroyed by the same way as the afflictions are destroyed, i.e., by meditation and by resolving the mind back into its primal cause, i.e., by attaining Samādhi.

Kaivalya is not a state of negation or annihilation as some foolishly imagine. It is perfect awareness. It is like Amalaka fruit in the palm of the hand. It is the highest state of bliss and knowledge. It is the highest goal in life. It is the eternal life in the Spirit or Pure Consciousness. It is the state of absolute peace, where cares, worries, fears, anxieties, tribulations, sorrows, vāsanās [samskāras] and trishnās [desires] do not torment the soul. It is the state of eternal sunshine and perennial joy. It is a state that cannot be adequately described in words. How can you describe the sweetness of sugarcandy? It is the state which is to realised and felt through aparokṣānubhūti [one's own experience] through vairāgya, sādhana and Samādhi.

When the Puruṣa has completed disconnected himself from the Prakṛti and its effects when he has realised that his happiness does not depend upon external objects, when he has recognised his own glory and independence, and when he feels his absolute freedom, then alone he has attained Kaivalya.

The Puruṣa realises His own native state of Divine Glory, Isolation or Absolute Independence. He has completely disconnected himself from the Prakṛti and its effects. He feels his absolute freedom and attains Kaivalya, the highest goal of Raja Yoga [Patañjali's Yoga]. All kleśas-karmas are destroyed now. The guṇas having fulfilled their objects of bhoga [experience] and apavarga [liberation] now entirely cease to act. He has simultaneous knowledge now. The past and future are blended into the present. Everything is 'now'. The sum total of all knowledge of the three worlds, of all secular sciences is nothing, nothing; it is mere husk when compared to the infinite knowledge of a Yogi who has attained Kaivalya. Glory, glory to such exalted Yogins. May their blessings be upon us all!"

STEP 8:

LOVING CONSCIOUSNESS

*"All you need is already within you, only you must
approach your Self with reverence and love."*
~ Nisargadatta Maharaj

On the spiritual journey to discover the Supreme Self within, we must be prepared to employ all our faculties to reach this lofty goal. We must employ our intellect in the study of helpful texts. We must employ our mind in meditation. And we must also employ our emotions. To ignore our emotions is to deny ourselves a powerful means for spiritual growth.

Love towards the higher is called 'devotion'. In devotion, the mind grows in its inherent powers with effortless ease. Our thoughts always gravitate easily and readily towards our love.

This step will help you cultivate love towards the Self. You will eventually come to realise that You are all-embracing love itself.

In order to get in touch with the feeling of love you can think of the person you love the most for a few minutes before the practice session, then use this same feeling of love in the meditation practice. This person may be your mother or father, a child, a boyfriend or girlfriend, a grandparent — choose the person that arouses in you the strongest feelings of love.

STEP 8: Meditation practise

YouTube link for Step 8 guided meditation:

https://youtu.be/BCZe41EUDes

also accessible via

https://www.youtube.com/@TheModernYogiLucy

Begin with the following techniques for quieting the mind:
- ❖ Steady posture
- ❖ Prayer/invocation
- ❖ Observing external sounds
- ❖ Body awareness
- ❖ Breath awareness
- ❖ Thought parade
- ❖ *Oṁ* chanting

When you are ready:
- ❖ Turn your attention away from thoughts towards your awareness — the Witness. The Witness is the Seer.
- ❖ Concentrate, in a relaxed manner, on loving the Seer.
- ❖ View the Seer as something sacred — and the most treasured.
- ❖ Continue loving the Seer.
- ❖ Relax and remain there.

What next?
- ❖ There is nothing else to be done.
- ❖ Just continue loving the Seer. The key is to be content with this. Don't seek more.
- ❖ After ten to twenty minutes, when you are ready, slowly bring the practice to an end.

STEP 8: Benefits

When devotion for the higher gains depth and sincerity, effortless awareness of one's true nature becomes constant and continuous.

Even if you find it difficult in the beginning, the important thing is not to give up.

After some days, weeks, or a few months you will start to feel something. At first it will be subtle, and you won't know what it is. You are beginning to know your Self as Eternal-Love-Bliss.

To the Yoga Scriptures!

The topics we will look at in Step 8 are:

- The fifth *Niyama*: *Īśvara praṇidhāna* (dedication to God/the Lord)
- *Īśvara* (God/the Lord) in Yoga
- *Oṁ*

The fifth *Niyama: Īśvara praṇidhāna* (dedication to God/the Lord)

Vyāsa defines *Īśvara praṇidhāna* as dedicating all one's activities to *Īśvara* (God or the Lord) the 'original teacher [of yoga]', without desire for fruit. This *niyama* can be compared to the *bhakti*-centred *karma-yoga* (selfless service) of *The Bhagavad Gītā* ('*karma*' here means action).

According to the laws of *karma*, all action, good or bad, when performed out of self-interest, plants a seed of reaction which must eventually bear fruit, good or bad, in this or a future life in accordance with the original deed. Through *Īśvara praṇidhāna*, one can avoid the cycle of *karmic* reaction by act-ing purely out of duty (*dharma*) rather than self-interest.

To implement *Īśvara praṇidhāna*, all our actions (*karmas*) — whether occurring within the practice of yoga or in every-day life with our families and at work — are done with certain inner attitudes. Below are some examples. The supreme goal of human life is always kept in view.

1) We do not act out of selfish desire for the fruits (re-sults) of our actions.
2) We are not attached to the outcome — we remain equipoised in both success and failure.
3) We surrender and offer the fruits of our actions to *Īśvara* or the Lord (God).
4) We see in our fellow beings the Self (*Puruṣa*). We feel that it is our own Self in essence in that particular form that we interact with.
5) We do not feel that we are the doer of the action or the enjoyer of its fruits. We are only the Witness (*Sākṣī*); *Prakṛti* in the form of the three *guṇas* does everything.
6) We see God in our fellow beings. When we serve them, we feel that we serve God.

The result of putting into practice *Īśvara praṇidhāna* is described in *Yoga-Sūtra* 2.45 as perfection of *samādhi*. Of all the boons resulting from the *yamas* and *niyamas*, it is only from *Īśvara praṇidhāna* that *samādhi*, the actual goal of yoga, is obtained.

How does it work?

The result of performing all our duties and actions in such a way is purity of the *citta*. It is only when the mind has reached sufficient purity that one is able to quiet the mind and succeed in the practice of meditation. Hence Patañjali includes *Īśvara praṇidhāna* as a necessary component of *kriyā-yoga* (see page 43).

This *niyama* results in *vairāgya* (detachment) because being equipoised, whatever the outcome, is the very core of *Īśvara praṇidhāna*.

Surrender to *Īśvara* is indispensable for the perfection of yoga. The yogi cultivates all the limbs of yoga but directs them toward God. In his 11th century commentary *Rāja-mārtaṇḍa*, Bhoja Rāja states that success is attained in this way because *Īśvara*, being pleased, removes the obstacles (*kleśas*) and awakens *samādhi*.

A significant section of *The Bhagavad Gītā* is devoted to this *sadhāna* (practice). For example:

"Perform action, O Arjuna, being steadfast in Yoga, abandoning attachment and balanced in success and failure. Evenness of mind is called Yoga." [verse 2.48]

"Having abandoned attachment to the fruits of the action, ever content, depending on nothing, he does not do anything though engaged in activity."
[verse 4.20]

Meaning:

It is the idea of agency, the idea 'I am the doer' that binds man to *saṁsāra* (cycle of birth/death). If this idea vanishes, action is no action at all. This is inaction in action. If you stand as a spectator or silent Witness of Nature's activities feeling that 'Nature does everything; I am the non-doer (*akarta*)'; if you identify yourself with the actionless Self, no matter what work or how much of it is done, action is no action at all. By such a practice and feeling, action loses its binding nature.

He or she who works for the well-being of others and who performs actions without egoism (sense of doer-ship) and attachment to the fruits, really does nothing at all, though ever engaged in activity as he or she has realised their identity with the Self which is beyond all activity.

Īśvara (God/the Lord) in Yoga

Puruṣa (Pure Awareness or Pure Consciousness), associated with the individual gross, subtle and causal bodies, is termed '*jīva*' or the 'limited individual'.

Puruṣa associated with the collective subtle body (the 'cosmic mind'), is termed '*Hiraṇyagarbha*'.

The term 'collective subtle body' relates to the entire subtle world, not just limited to humans. The whole mental world of thoughts, ideation, and so on of all beings, right from the unicellular stretching upwards, becomes the subtle body of *Īśvara*. Our subtle body is part of this total.

According to Hariharānanda, *Hiraṇyagarbha* is "the omniscient and all-pervading Creator", i.e. the creator, maintainer and destroyer of the universe; and "the original exponent of Yoga Philosophy."

That there is a God (*Īśvara*) who is described as creator, maintainer and destroyer, is not a view found in the *Sāmkhyakārikā*, but it can be found in the *Sāṃkhyasūtra* (a 15th century text).

The following are some of the important differences between the *jīva* (individual) and *Īśvara*:

- *Jīva* possesses limited knowledge; *Īśvara* possesses boundless knowledge.
- *Jīva* is limited by time and space; *Īśvara* is all-pervading and eternal.
- *Īśvara* is the all-powerful Lord, the controller of the whole cosmos, whereas the *jīva* is limited in power.
- *Īśvara* controls *Prakṛti* and her evolutes and is ever aware of His/Her true nature as Pure Consciousness, whereas the *jīva* is ignorant of his or her own true nature.
- The *jīva*, bound by ignorance and the effects of *Prakṛti*, strives for liberation. Since *Īśvara*, has no ignorance, and is ever free of bondage, there is no need at all for liberation.

• In spite of being the creator, sustainer and destroyer of worlds and being ever engaged in activity, *Īśvara* is detached from His/Her actions because of the Self-Knowledge that is natural to Him/Her. The *jīva*, being ignorant of his or her real nature, identifies with the conditionings of the gross, subtle and causal bodies, considers him or herself to be the doer and enjoyer, and is thus a bound individual.

Oṁ

The word *Oṁ* consists of three letters: A, U, and M. Due to the rules of Sanskrit grammar the first two letters (A-U) joined together becomes 'O'. Diversified objects, designated by names, constitute the entire universe.

Phonetically, "A" is the basic sound that is produced by a

human being anywhere in the world, when he tries to make a sound by opening the mouth. In most languages "A" is also the first letter of the alphabet. When a sound is produced by closing the mouth, what comes out is the sound "M". The letter "U" is inserted in between to indicate all sounds in between. Thus, *Oṁ* comprising the letters "A", "U", and "M" includes all sounds and therefore, all letters and all words of all languages and dialects.

All objects are but names and all names are words. Words, being made of letters, are nothing but letters, and letters are sounds. The Lord being everything, His/Her name should include every name. As *Oṁ* is a word that indicates all objects, *Oṁ* becomes the name of *Īśvara*.

CONSOLIDATION OF STEPS 5 to 8

*"Abandoning all limited concepts, abandoning
even the division between the worshipper and
the worshipped, worship the Self by the Self.
Be at peace, pure, free from cravings."*
~ THE YOGA VASISTHA

To reach the peak we need to climb gradually and patiently. To reach the formless, we still need the three bodies (or five sheaths). Our various *sādhanas* (practices) — *Yama, Niyma, Āsana, Prāṇāyāma*, etc., cannot be neglected.

For how long should one practice?

The answer lies in *Yoga-Sūtra* 1.14:

- *Dīrgha-kāla*: continuously.
- *Nairantarya*: without any gap or break for a long duration.
- *Satkāra*: with much devotion. One should have deep respect for the practice. Only then will the Self reveal itself to the seeker.
- *Āsevitaḥ*: one must practice with great care, attention and with a firm resolve in order for the *prajñā-Saṁskāras* (see page 97) to take root at a deep level.

As your meditation practice develops, you will be able to spend less time on the first part of the practice aimed at quieting the mind. It will all depend on how your mind is on a given day. If you find yourself having many thought agitations, then it is helpful to spend sufficient time on watching the breath and so on.

Regarding the question of how long to meditate: even 30 minutes of daily meditation practice is beneficial.

If you strongly desire liberation it is recommended that you practice for a longer duration, at least one hour and if possible two hours a day, in order to progress more rapidly.

However, this should not be forced, especially if you are relatively new to meditation. Then begin with 30 minutes of meditation practice (once or preferably twice a day) and gradually, carefully, increase the duration.

When you are not practising seated meditation, you should still aim to continuously identify with the Eternal Self.

In his book *Towards the Goal Supreme*, Swami Virajananda of the Ramakrishna Order discusses the necessity for sustained self-effort. He writes:

"Resolve firmly, 'I will realise God through my own efforts by doing spiritual practices' and go on steadfastly practising Japa [mantra repetition] and meditation, seated in proper posture, for at least two hours every morning and evening, for three or four years — and see if you succeed or not."

FROM DUALITY TO NON-DUALITY

"In seeking you discover that you are neither the body nor mind, and the love of the Self in you is for the Self in all. The two are one. The consciousness in you and the consciousness in me, apparently two, really one."
~ Nisargadatta Maharaj

In this last chapter we will dive deep into the rabbit hole of non-duality. This is the school of philosophy called *Advaita Vedānta* ('*Vedānta*'). It represents a radical departure from the dualistic philosophy of *Sāṅkhya* and Yoga.

As spiritual seekers, it is perhaps more helpful to view *Vedānta* not as a radically different path, but rather the path which takes *Sāṅkhya* to its ultimately glorious conclusion.

Of all the philosophical systems *Sāṅkhya* is considered to be the most ancient root of all Indian schools of thought.

At the beginning of the Ramakrishna Order's commentary on the *Sāṁkhya Kārikā* of Īśvara Kṛṣṇa, it is remarked:

"Today Vedānta rules the roost... but it must be noted that Vedānta takes off to ethereal heights only from the granite platform provided by Sāṅkhya."

"Sāṅkhya reduces everything to two entities — Prakṛti and Puruṣa. What Vedānta does is to integrate these two further into one splendid all-comprehensive Unity."

Vedānta, the teachings found in the *Upaniṣads*, expounds the great truth that the Self or Seer alone is the sole Reality.

The Self is Infinite-Eternal-Being-Awareness-Bliss. It is given various names such as *Puruṣa*, Self, Seer, Witness (*Sākṣī*), *Brahman*, Spirit, God.

We are all that one Self. The awareness that is in you is the same awareness in me and in every other living creature, big and small.

Pure flawless awareness is your true nature right now, it is not something that needs to be gained. Everything else that can be perceived by the senses (the 'seen') is an illusion or appearance. This includes everything made from the three *guṇas* — the body, mind and intellect, and external world.

There is one Reality — the Pure Consciousness (or Pure Awareness), although it appears as many. But behind the appearance of the world of multiplicity, there is oneness. Similar to the experience of a film, only the screen is real, remaining totally unaffected by the various scenes that are projected onto it.

The meditation practice given here is inspired from the following verse in the *Aṣṭāvakra Gītā*:

> *"Like bubbles in the sea,*
> *All the worlds arise in you.*
> *Know you are the Self.*
> *Know you are one.*
> *Let yourself dissolve."*

Please read the following instructions and then proceed. I have not provided a guided meditation for this chapter.

Meditation practise instructions: Ocean of Awareness

Begin with the following techniques for quieting the mind:
- Steady posture
- Prayer/invocation
- Observing external sounds
- Body awareness
- Breath awareness
- Thought parade
- *Oṁ* chanting

When you are ready:
- Turn your attention away from thoughts towards awareness, the Self.
- From the core of your being — your heart centre — visualize your awareness slowly expanding outward in all directions. Allow it to encompass the entire physical universe: all the planets, stars, and galaxies. This is an infinite ocean that knows no boundaries.
- Acknowledge that all objects (seen and unseen), including your own body and that of others, the Earth, moon, and stars, all appear to rise and fall in that awareness. Like bubbles in the sea, they are all impermanent and eventually collapse back into their true nature of Pure Consciousness (Pure Awareness).
- Contemplate for a moment the highest truth that nothing is created for all of eternity. Perfect homogeneous oneness is all there was, is, and ever will be.
- Now drop even this thought.
- Turn your attention inwards, away from the world, body, and mind (all mental activity) and towards awareness.

❖ Give attention to awareness alone.
❖ If thoughts come, do not try to complete them, just turn your attention back to the Subject.
❖ Love awareness, the Seer, as something sacred.
❖ Continue loving the Seer. You are That.
❖ Relax and remain there, without thought, in the peace that passeth all understanding.

Benefit of this practice

This practice will help you to assimilate the profound truth that there is no objective universe apart from You: Pure Awareness. The entire physical universe is nothing but an appearance in You.

This step will help you to 'see' beyond the names and forms. You will still visibly see the world, yet you will be able to discriminate between the Real and the apparently real.

Swami Sivananda provides the following guidance:

"When you look at an object behold Brahman [another name for the Self] which is the one essence and abandon the form as it is illusory and unreal. Have the same attitude towards the objects which pertain to the other senses."

The Reality of the entire universe is Pure Awareness-Bliss.

The Reality of you is the Self which is Pure Awareness-Bliss.

There is only one Self.

***Tat Tvam Asi* — You Are That.**